Masterir Primary Physical Education

Mastering Primary Teaching series

Edited by Judith Roden and James Archer

The *Mastering Primary Teaching* series provides an insight into the core principles underpinning each of the subjects of the Primary National Curriculum, thereby helping student teachers to 'master' the subjects. This in turn will enable new teachers to share this mastery in their teaching. Each book follows the same sequence of chapters, which has been specifically designed to assist trainee teachers to capitalize on opportunities to develop pedagogical excellence. These comprehensive guides introduce the subject and help trainees know how to plan and teach effective and inspiring lessons that make learning irresistible. Examples of children's work and case studies are included to help exemplify what is considered to be best and most innovative practice in primary education. The series is written by leading professionals, who draw on their years of experience to provide authoritative guides to the primary curriculum subject areas.

Also available in the series

Mastering Primary English, Wendy Jolliffe and David Waugh

Mastering Primary Languages, Paula Ambrossi and Darnelle Constant-Shepherd

Mastering Primary Music, Ruth Atkinson

Mastering Primary Science, Amanda McCrory and Kenna Worthington

Forthcoming in the series

Mastering Primary Art and Design, Peter Gregory, Claire March and Suzy Tutchell

Mastering Primary Computing, Graham Parton and Christine Kemp-Hall

Mastering Primary Design and Technology, Gill Hope

Mastering Primary Geography, Anthony Barlow and Sarah Whitehouse

Mastering Primary History, Karin Doull, Christopher Russell and Alison Hales

Mastering Primary Mathematics, TBC

Mastering Primary Religious Education, Maria James and Julian Stern

Also available from Bloomsbury

Developing Teacher Expertise, edited by Margaret Sangster

Readings for Reflective Teaching in Schools, edited by Andrew Pollard

Reflective Teaching in Schools, Andrew Pollard

Mastering Primary Physical Education

Kristy Howells with Alison Carney, Neil Castle and Rich Little

Bloomsbury Academic
An imprint of Bloomsbury Publishing Plc

B L O O M S B U R Y
LONDON · OXFORD · NEW YORK · NEW DELHI · SYDNEY

Bloomsbury Academic

An imprint of Bloomsbury Publishing Plc

50 Bedford Square
London
WC1B 3DP
UK

1385 Broadway
New York
NY 10018
USA

www.bloomsbury.com

**BLOOMSBURY and the Diana logo are trademarks
of Bloomsbury Publishing Plc**

First published 2018

British Library Cataloguing-in-Publication Data
A catalogue record for this book is available from the British Library.

ISBN: HB: 978-1-4742-9688-5
PB: 978-1-4742-9687-8
ePDF: 978-1-4742-9689-2
ePub: 978-1-4742-9690-8

Library of Congress Cataloging-in-Publication Data
A catalog record for this book is available from the Library of Congress.

Series: Mastering Primary Teaching

Cover design by Anna Berzovan
Cover image © iStock (miakievy/molotovcoketail)

Typeset by Deanta Global Publishing Services, Chennai, India
Printed and bound in Great Britain

To find out more about our authors and books visit www.bloomsbury.com. Here
you will find extracts, author interviews, details of forthcoming events and the
option to sign up for our newsletters.

Contents

List of Figures

List of Tables

Series Editors' Foreword

A long and varied experience of working with beginner and experienced teachers in primary schools has informed this series since its conception. Over the last thirty years there have been many changes in practice in terms of teaching and learning in primary and early years education. Significantly, since the implementation of the first National Curriculum in 1989 the aim has been to bring best practice in primary education to all state schools in England and Wales. As time has passed, numerous policy decisions have altered the detail and emphasis of the delivery of the primary curriculum. However, there has been little change in the belief that pupils in the primary and early years phases of education should receive a broad, balanced curriculum based on traditional subjects.

Recent Ofsted subject reports and notably the Cambridge Primary Review indicate that rather than the ideal being attained, in many schools, the emphasis on English and mathematics has not only depressed the other subjects of the primary curriculum, but also narrowed the range of strategies used for the delivery of the curriculum. The amount of time allocated to subject sessions in ITE courses has dramatically reduced which may also account for this narrow diet in pedagogy.

The vision for this series of books was borne out of our many years of experience with student teachers. As a result, we believe that the series is well designed to equip trainee and beginner teachers to master the art of teaching in the primary phase. This series of books aims to introduce current and contemporary practices associated with the whole range of subjects within the Primary National Curriculum and religious education. It also goes beyond this by providing beginner teachers with the knowledge and understanding required to achieve mastery of each subject. In doing so, each book in the series highlights contemporary issues such as assessment and inclusion which are the key areas that even the most seasoned practitioner is still grappling with in light of the introduction of the new Primary Curriculum. In agreement with the results attached with these books, we believe that students who work in schools and progress onto their Newly Qualified Teacher (NQT) year will be able to make a significant contribution to the provision in their school, especially in foundation subjects.

Readers will find great support within each one of these books. Each book in the series will inform and provide the opportunity for basic mastery of each of the subjects, namely English, mathematics, science, physical education, music, history, geography, design and technology computing and religious education. They will discover the essence of each subject in terms of its philosophy, knowledge and skills. Readers will also be inspired by the enthusiasm for each subject revealed by the subject authors who are experts in their field. They will discover many and varied strategies for making each subject 'come alive' for their pupils and they should become more confident about teaching across the whole range of subjects represented in the primary and early years curriculum.

Primary teaching in the state sector is characterized by a long history of pupils being taught the whole range of the primary curriculum by one teacher. Although some schools may employ specialists to deliver some subjects of the curriculum, notably physical education, music or science, for example, it is more usual for the whole curriculum to be delivered to a class by their class teacher. This places a potentially enormous burden on beginner teachers no matter which route they enter teaching. The burden is especially high on those entering through employment-based routes and for those who aim to become inspiring primary teachers. There is much to learn!

The term 'mastery' is generally considered to relate to knowledge and understanding of a subject which incorporates the 'how' of teaching as well as the 'what'. Although most entrants to primary teaching will have some experience of the primary curriculum as a pupil, very few will have experienced the breadth of the curriculum or may have any understanding of the curriculum which reflects recent trends in teaching and learning within the subject. The primary curriculum encompasses a very broad range of subjects each of which has its own knowledge base, skills and ways of working. Unsurprisingly, very few new entrants into the teaching profession hold mastery of all the interrelated subjects. Indeed for the beginner teacher it may well be many years before full mastery of all aspects of the primary curriculum is achieved. The content of the primary curriculum has changed significantly, notably in some foundation subjects, such as history and music. So although beginner teachers might hold fond memories of these subjects from their own experience of primary education, the content of the subject may well have changed significantly over time and may incorporate different emphases.

This series, Mastering Primary Teaching, aims to meet the needs of those who, reflecting the desire for mastery over each subject, want to know more. This is a tall order. Nevertheless, we believe that the pursuit of development should always be rewarded, which is why we are delighted to have so many experts sharing their well-developed knowledge and passion for the subjects featured in each book. The vision for this series is to provide support for those who are beginning their teaching career, who may not feel fully secure in their subject knowledge, understanding and skill. In addition, the series also aims to provide a reference point for beginner teachers to always be able to go back to support them in the important art of teaching.

Intending primary teachers, in our experience, have a thirst for knowledge about the subject that they will be teaching. They want to 'master' new material and ideas in a range of subjects. They aim to gain as much knowledge as they can of the subjects they will be teaching, in some of which the beginner teachers may lack in confidence or may be scared of because of their perceived lack of familiarity with some subjects and particularly how they are delivered in primary schools. Teaching the primary curriculum can be one of the most rewarding experiences. We believe that this series will help the beginner teachers to unlock the primary curriculum in a way that ensures they establish themselves as confident primary practitioners.

Judith Roden

James Archer

June 2017

How to Use This Book

This book is one of twelve books that together help form a truly innovative series that is aimed to support your development. Each book follows the same format and chapter sequence. There is an emphasis throughout the book on providing information about the teaching and learning of physical education. You will find a wealth of information within each chapter that will help you to understand the issues, problems and opportunities that teaching the subject can provide you as a developing practitioner in the subject. Crucially, each chapter provides opportunities for you to reflect upon important points linked to your development of the in order that you may master the teaching of physical education. As a result you get to develop confidence in the teaching of primary physical education. There really is something for everyone within each chapter.

Each chapter has been carefully designed to help you to develop your knowledge of the subject systematically. Chapter objectives clearly signpost the content of each chapter and these will help you to familiarize yourself with important aspects of the subject and will orientate you in preparation for reading the chapter. The regular 'Pause for Thought' points offer questions and activities for you to reflect on important aspects of the subject. Each 'Pause for Thought' point provides you with an opportunity to enhance your learning beyond merely reading the chapter. These will sometimes ask you to consider your own experience and what you already know about the teaching of the subject. Others will require you to critique aspects of good practice presented as case studies or research. To benefit fully from reading this book, you need to be an active participant. Sometimes you are asked to make notes on your response to questions and ideas and then to revisit these later on in your reading. While it would be possible for you to skim through the opportunities for reflection or to give only cursory attention to the questions and activities which aim to facilitate deeper reflection than might otherwise be the case, we strongly urge you to engage with the pause-for-thought activities. It is our belief that it is through these moments that most of your transformational learning will occur. At the end of each chapter, you will find a summary of the main points from the chapter, along with suggestions for further reading.

We passionately believe that learners of all ages learn best when they work with others, so we encourage you, if possible, to work with another person, sharing your ideas and perspectives. The book also would be ideal for group study within a university or school setting.

This book has been authored by Kristy Howells with Alison Carney, Neil Castle and Rich Little, all of whom are experienced and highly regarded professionals in their subject area. They are strong voices within the primary physical education community. By reading this book you will be able to benefit from their rich knowledge, understanding and experience. When using this, ensure that you are ready to learn from some of the greats in primary physical education.

Acknowledgements

We would like to recognize and acknowledge the contribution that each author has made to this book. Kristy Howells led the writing and brought the whole book together; she wrote Chapter 1 – An Introduction to Primary Physical Education, Chapter 5 – Developing Curiosity and Physical Development, as well as writing Chapter 7 – Observing and Assessing Children in Physical Education. Alison Carney wrote Chapter 8 – Practical Issues in Physical Education. Neil Castle wrote both Chapters 2 and 3 – Current Developments in Physical Education, as well as Physical Education as an Irresistible Activity. Rich Little wrote Chapter 4 – Physical Education as a Practical Activity and Chapter 6 – Skills to Develop in Physical Education. We would like to acknowledge our students, especially our Schools Direct students, who fed back to us all, on our chapters as we devised and trialled, especially our pause for thought moments, in a wonderful spiral of research informing teaching and teaching informing research.

As a team we would also like to acknowledge all the children, parents and teachers who have given their permission to allow us to share their photographs and their examples of movements within Physical Education and Physical Development lessons. We would specifically like to acknowledge the children from River Primary School and the children from White Cliffs Primary School College for Arts, who also shared examples of lessons plans as well as appearing in our photographs. We would like to acknowledge and thank Jenny Hill for contributing her photographs. We would also like to thanks our own children for participating within our photographs to illustrate movement, as well as our friends' children who also appear throughout the book, with whom our Physical Education illustrations become alive.

We dedicate this book to J. D.; Paul, Alistair, Lewis; Helen, Samuel, Benjamin; Jo, Evie, Harvey, and Sam in appreciation for their fabulous support that they have given us throughout our writing and editing of this book.

Chapter 1
An Introduction to Primary Physical Education

Chapter objectives

- What is primary physical education?
- What is sustained activity and how can we ensure this occurs?
- Why physical education should be taught and what is the value of physical education?
- What does it mean to be physically educated?
- How can physical education contribute to a child's whole education?

Introduction

This chapter will enable you to understand the importance of primary physical education and how you, as the teacher/practitioner within the educational setting, can inspire and motivate your children to physically develop, be physically active and become physically educated.

Pause for thought – *Thinking about the value of physical education:*

What is the point of physical education?

What do children learn from physical education?

How would you explain to a child *why* we are doing physical education today?

What is primary physical education?

Primary physical education has three parts that contribute to the overall activity that may occur within a school or an early years setting. These include physical education, physical development and physical activity, and these will each be examined individually.

Physical education

Physical education has previously been defined by Howells (2012) as a place within the curriculum where attitudes and interests can be fostered and an understanding of the importance of physical activity, diet and healthy lifestyles can be shared with and developed within the children. It is a place where passion and where an enthusiasm and a love for movement can be imparted to the children and a place where lifelong physical activity can be developed. Howells (2011) proposed that physical education is beyond just being active and providing exercise opportunities. Authors such as Rink et al. (2010) proposed that 'Physical Education programs are now designed to prepare students to be physically active' (p. 49) so that children can be physically active both within physical education lessons and outside the class.

Sallis and Owen (1999) suggested that physical education lessons could be the place that provides the main opportunity for physical activity for many young people. Murphy and Ní Chroinin (2011) agreed and highlighted that physical education lessons were a vital part of the child's life in school, as physical education lessons may be one of the only places within the curriculum where a child can 'learn in and through movement' (p. 142). However, primary physical education is not just about being physically active, but about developing and educating the child physically, in a holistic manner (Doherty and Brennan, 2007), and about developing basic skills and movements (Jess and Dewar, 2004). Hellison and Templin (1991) suggested that social learning should be a particular focus within physical education lessons. Within the primary school, children are at a stage where habits, likes and dislikes are formed (Howells, 2012); therefore, physical education is more than just the act of being physically active. Yelling et al. (2000), prior to Howells (2012), suggested that physical activity was 'only one consideration of Physical Education lessons and the National Curriculum for Physical Education' (p. 62). The aims of the National Curriculum for physical education in England (DfEE/QCA, 1999) encompassed promotion of the children's spiritual, moral, social, cultural and academic development.

Since the introduction of the 'new' Primary National Curriculum (DfE, 2014) in England, there has been a shift in both the purpose of study for physical education and the aims. The purpose of study now expects you to provide a 'high-quality physical education curriculum' that 'inspires all children to succeed and excel in competitive sport and other physically-demanding activities. It should provide opportunities for children to become confident in a way which supports their health and fitness. Opportunities to compete in sport and other activities build character and help to embed values such as fairness and respect' (DfE, 2013, p. 198). The aims revolve around a healthy lifestyle perspective, with all children developing competence to excel in a broad range of physical activities, sustaining physical activity and engaging in competitive sports and activities.

Physical education, historically within England, used to be a very traditional lesson in which discrete sports were played. These were mainly traditional games that varied across the country depending on where you lived to being more, for example, rugby focused versus football focused (Figure 1.1). These activities were very competitive, almost exclusive and elitist. There was a great deal of running, in particular cross-country running, and the focus was on those children who could.

Figure 1.1 Football-focused traditional game

Now that the 'old' National Curriculum's activity areas and breadth of study have been removed, there are no longer the requirements of dance activities, games activities, gymnastics activities, swimming activities and water safety, athletics activities and outdoor and adventurous activities (DfEE/QCA, 1999). There are suggested activities that could be used, but they are not compulsory, allowing for much more freedom within the lessons, which will help children to learn movement skills and concepts in more detail. The focus within physical education now is on developing fundamental movement skills (which will be discussed in more detail in Chapter 5). There has now been an increase in the number of key words beginning with the letter 'c' to 5cs for children aged up to 7; these include developing competence, confidence, coordination, cooperation and undertaking challenge. For children aged 7–11 there are an extra 3cs on top of those for the young children and these include communicating, collaborating (Figure 1.2) and competing (DfE, 2013). The progression with age allows for the basic movements to be developed from movements completed in isolation to a combination of movements (Figure 1.3). It allows for simple movement patterns to be developed into ranges of patterns and tactics of defending and attacking that would evolve into a variety of modified competitive games. This progression of transferable skills, and the phrase 'enjoy communicating, collaborating and competing' being used for the first time in the curriculum, will allow more children to be successful both individually and within a team setting, to be excited about physical education and to enjoy their lessons.

Figure 1.2 Key Stage 2 – children communicating and collaborating within an outdoor and adventure activities lesson

Figure 1.3 Children completing combination movements of a triple jump

(The children have joined together a hop, a skip/leap and a jump which they had practiced in isolation to make the combined movement of a triple jump. The girls in Figure 1.3 are in different stages of the triple jump. The one on the left is starting in the hop and the one on the right is transitioning from the hop to the skip/leap.)

Physical development

> ## Pause for thought – *to write down your thoughts before going on*:
>
> What do you think Physical Development is in the early years?
>
> What would you want your children to achieve as goals of early movement?
>
> Do any of them begin with the letter c?

Physical development is a term mainly found within the early years setting, but does and will also include reception classes (those aged 4–5 years) within primary school settings. Physical development itself is one of the seven areas of learning and development identified in the Early Years Foundation Stage Statutory Framework in England (DfE, 2014). It is regarded as one of the prime areas, alongside communication and language and personal, social and emotional development. The prime areas are interwoven and interconnected within the specific areas of literacy, numeracy and understanding the world and expressive arts and design. The specific requirements of physical development include ensuring that young children have opportunities to be 'active and interactive' (p. 8, DfE, 2014). The early learning goals for physical development can be summarized into the '**3cs**', which include moving with control, coordination and confidence, the later with particular relationship to the children's movement within space, both their own immediate space and the general space they share with others. Therefore, you need to plan for physical development within structured and unstructured learning that includes developing and supporting children's learning of moving with control, coordination and confidence. This can be using small or large equipment, and using both indoor and outdoor environments. The links between the early learning goals and physical development will be extended in Chapter 5.

Physical development is the way in which children develop physically and master skills; this can be within both structured and unstructured activities. There is a large physical strand to the Early Years Foundation Stage which is viewed in a variety of ways such as how children develop large motor skills (gross motor skills) or small motor skills (fine motor skills). This is evident from the early learning goals that refer both to large body movements such as skipping, jumping and hopping (Figure 1.4) and to small body movements such as writing and using the correct grip. This highlights the impact of learning physically; it is not just a lesson, but a journey that the child goes on and that is supported through opportunities to explore, enquire and investigate. These opportunities are the focus you need to master to ensure children can physically develop.

(In the picture on the right-hand side the child at the right back of the photograph is using her hands in a closed fist shape which is helping her with control and balance of her hopping. The child at the front of the photograph is using her hands in a crossed-over position, again to help her try and keep balance.)

There are numerous physical development milestones; the ones that are focused on within reception classes in the primary school setting, for those aged 4–5, are linked to both fine and gross motor skills including (as described by Meggit 2006) jumping on one foot, walking backwards, cutting paper with safety scissors and printing. However, it is important to note that children develop at different rates and

Figure 1.4 Children jumping and hopping within gymnastics

therefore may need opportunities to support and develop these milestones within the school setting. Do not assume that they can undertake these prior to their arriving at school. In order to master physical development, Almond and Lambden (2016) propose promoting purposeful physical play and the Welsh Assembly Government (2008) advises practitioners that they need to 'provide active, experiential learning through careful planning, organising, facilitating, challenging, observing, interacting, intervening and evaluating'.

Pause for thought – *A scenario-based question:*

You have just been awarded a large sum of money for equipment to enhance Physical Development within your class to help develop their physical skills. What will you buy and why?

Physical activity

Primary schools often have physical activity policies that are read alongside their physical education policies. These policies are designed to present the aims of the school and to recognize that physical activity is wider than just physical education and to recognize the opportunities presented to children within the school to enjoy physical activity, to promote physical activity and to encourage positive choice, including those at play time, within curriculum and after school provision. Within the policy the provision, resources, equipment, funding, assessment, additional support for children with special educational needs (SEN), for example, coordination difficulties as well as leadership and management roles need to be identified. Policies may also include dress codes and health and safety procedures. The policies are usually reviewed every two years and are published online and are linked to Ofsted's School self-evaluation form.

Physical activity has previously been proposed by Howells (2012) as having numerous definitions, as being a complex behaviour variable and as being difficult to measure in children, especially in young children. According to Winsley and Armstrong (2005), physical activity varies 'from day to day, in intensity, frequency and duration and consists of both unavoidable and variable activities' (p. 65). Children also find it difficult to describe their physical activity levels (Kolle et al., 2009) due to the fact that children frequently move from one intensity level to another and the length of time spent within each intensity level may be very sporadic within both structured and unstructured physical activity. Physical activities have several intensity levels: static, low level, moderate and then vigorous level.

A recent infographic campaign by the Department of Health in 2016 has been linked to previous work from the chief medical officers (CMOs) in the UK (2011), who suggested that babies and children from birth to 5 years should be active for at least 180 minutes per day. The 2016 slogan that is being used is 'Every Movement Counts' and the Department of Health (in the UK) highlights that these movements could include playing, crawling, walking and jumping (Figure 1.5). The CMOs (2011) and also Almond and Lambden (2016) proposed for young children that physical activity should be encouraged from birth through floor-based play and water-based activities (Figure 1.6). They proposed that all under-5s should minimize the amount of time spent being sedentary for extended periods of time.

Examples of physical activity that would meet the guidelines are mostly unstructured active play, but also include more structured play such as energetic activities of climbing on climbing frames or running or riding bikes (Figures 1.7 and 1.8). In the new surge of popularity this may now include scootering (as per the new infographic), though it would be proposed by the author of this chapter that children be strongly encouraged to use both feet when scootering (Figure 1.9) by

Figure 1.5 Kaidee walking (with a little help from the chair to stop) and crawling

Figure 1.6 Water-based play and floor-based play at the beach

Figure 1.7 Cycling at different ages (Samuel 9 yrs left, then Benjamin 7 yrs and Jack 5 yrs right.)

Figure 1.8 Emma running, and how she loves running!

Figure 1.9 Evie scootering

encouraging them to swap feet and to also use their whole foot as if they would when walking, or running, to ensure that scootering does not impact on their fundamental movement skills and limit children's ability to undertake other locomotor activities. The CMOs (2011) emphasized that the benefits of young children being physically active and moving are that it contributes to the whole development of the child, by developing their motor skills of movement and coordination, improving their cognitive development and by supporting learning of social skills.

For children aged 5–18 the Department of Health's (2016) campaign is, 'Be physically active, sit less, move more.' Again they have linked back to the CMOs' (2011) report that suggested that physical activity for children and young children should be 60 minutes per day and can be spread throughout the day and all activities should make the children breathe faster and feel warmer. The examples of physical activity that are promoted and could be completed by children and young people (5–18) include playing, running, walking, swimming, skating, skipping, climbing, cycling, sport, working out, dancing and active travelling (meaning walking or cycling to school, rather than taking the bus). Plus, the most important activity area for us that is interestingly recognized and listed is physical education. The benefits that are recognized in the infographic are that physical activity builds confidence and social skills, develops coordination, improves concentration and learning, strengthens muscles and bones, improves health and fitness, maintains a healthy weight, improves sleep and enhances feelings (i.e. makes you feel good).

Pause for thought – *Thinking about how you inspire your children:*

What physical activity do you do yourself? How would you share your experiences to motivate, engage, encourage and inspire your children to be physically active?

How would all of your educational setting or school encourage *all* children and staff to participate in Physical Education and physical activity within the school setting? What photographs or newspaper reports or articles could you use to inspire the children and staff?

What is sustained activity and how can we ensure this occurs?

The concept of sustained physical activity comes from both the Primary Education curriculum for England (DfE 2013) and the Early Years Foundations Stage framework for England (DfE, 2014). Howells (2016), however, highlighted the difficulties within both curricula, stating that 'there is a focus on sustained physical activity, but there is no curriculum guidance about what sustained physical activity is and how it is defined'. Howells and Meehan (2015) investigated the perceptions and attitudes of teachers and early years' practitioners of physical activity (locally in the South East, Kent, Medway and London) and reported on confidence levels and found that, although physical activity was regarded as important, early years' practitioners, in particular, were less confident in knowing how to sustain physical activity within their settings. The findings also highlighted for both primary teachers and early years practitioners that children often repeated the same set of physical activities and it was concluded that more support was needed in delivering sustained physical activity. Almond and Lambden (2016) offer guidance in conducting sustained activity sessions when children are engrossed in purposeful play for longer than 10 minutes.

For children aged 0–5 the National Health Service (NHS, 2013) guidance suggests that children should not be inactive for long periods and specifies that children should experience light and energetic activities. For children aged 5–17 the Department of Health (DH, 2005) and the World Health Organization (WHO, 2010) recommend that children be physically active at a moderate-to-vigorous intensity level for 60 minutes per day. This intensity level is when the children are breathing hard and sweating. Green (2002) emphasized how important physical education lessons could be as a 'suitable vehicle for encouragement of a lifestyle which is both healthy and physically active' (p. 97). The NHS (2011) guidelines offer recommendations for primary-aged children that could be completed within the school setting or on the way to the school setting. These include push-ups, gymnastics, sit-ups, swinging on playground equipment, rock climbing (Figure 1.10) and games such as tug of war. To ensure sustainability of the activities, larger equipment for activities such as rock climbing and swinging on playground equipment could be provided through the use of the primary school physical education and sport premium funding currently available (at the time of writing) from the Government 2016 Budget, to all primary schools until 2020. A fund of £320 million per year would be available from September 2017 to help schools support more active children, by developing quality and breadth of

Figure 1.10 Children engaged in rock climbing

physical education, physical activity and sport available within the school setting. The NHS (2011) also suggested activities that could be sustained again within the school setting, especially in the playground during break time, and through the use of small equipment or with no equipment that would help children's bone strengthening, which is an important aspect of physical activities. These activities include hopscotch, skipping and jumping, skipping with a rope, running, gymnastics, football, volleyball and tennis. These could all be ensured through the putting out of small equipment during play/break times and also by mid-day supervisors or staff supervising children on the playground to prompt children with ideas of what activities to undertake.

Other factors that are needed to ensure that sustained activity is being undertaken within primary physical education are considering how often within gymnastics activities do children queue for equipment, or queue for their turn within a striking and fielding activity. Do they need to queue? Could the children be undertaking smaller-sized games or larger circuits to allow them more time on different pieces of equipment, to ensure they are developing physically, enhancing and developing their understanding of the skills that is needed for the activity? Another consideration is the amount of teacher talk and the length of instructions. Howells (2015) identified that the pace of the lesson is key to keeping the children engaged, positive and inspired. If the children meet these three parameters then they will be more likely to be more active within the lesson. McKenzie and Kahan (2004) also found that they were able to increase physical activity levels within the physical education lesson by 3 minutes, which is an impact of 18 per cent of the whole physical education lesson! Therefore, it is important to be aware of what you are doing and how this may impact on the lesson and to plan (with timings on plans) for the children to undertake activities for periods of time that will help sustain physical activity.

Why should physical education be taught and what is the value of physical education?

Simons-Morton et al., as early as 1994, emphasized the importance of physical education lessons for those who do little or no physical activity outside of these lessons or outside of school. They suggested that substantial amounts of physical activity could occur within physical education lessons. Yet, according to Howells (2011), physical education 'should encompass individual physical development, health and wellbeing' (p. 119) and had a crucial role in primary school education as it was more than just simply providing exercising opportunities for every child. Within primary school, children are at a stage where habits, likes and dislikes are formed (Howells 2012); therefore physical education is more than just the act of being physically active. The aims of the 'old' National Curriculum for physical education in England and Wales (DfEE/QCA, 1999) encompassed promotion of the children's spiritual, moral, social, cultural and academic performance. Similar aims can be seen in the new curriculum (DfE, 2013) in the form of developing communication and collaboration skills *(social, moral and cultural)*; being able to cope with competing *(moral and spiritual)*, and experiencing increasingly challenging, situations *(cognitive, academic, moral and social)*; and evaluating and recognizing success *(cognitive, academic, social)*. Doherty and Brennan (2007) supported this notion that physical education develops a child holistically through a physical means.

Primary physical education is for some children the first place that they experience structured physical activity. Therefore, it is vital as teachers and practitioners that we make physical education lessons a safe, fun, purposeful and engaging environment that children will want to return to. It is recommended that physical education is a subject to ensure that you do teach and not to give it up for someone else to take during your planning, preparation and assessment release time. The reason for not releasing it is that you and the children will experience a classroom setting that is unfamiliar to the one they are in on a daily basis, whether that be the indoor hall, or the playground or the field. The children need to see you within this unusual learning environment as a positive role model, as this experience is vital to their development (Howells, 2007) and the notion of feeling safe. It has been reported by Blair and Capel (2008) that some generalist primary teachers do not view themselves as being confident in teaching physical education; however, a generalist can easily become a specialist by working alongside more experienced others, undertaking CPD and having a willingness to have a go, and embrace their potential fear and begin to master physical education. If you are not in the lesson, you will miss those moments when Gloria throws a hammer for miles, when Jonny performs a cartwheel with his legs pointing towards the ceiling for the first time (Figure 1.11), when Freddie jumps

Figure 1.11 'Jonny' cartwheeling with his toes towards the ceiling (or with at least one foot and toes pointed, as is captured in the photo)

into the swimming pool without holding his nose. Those are magical moments that you need to experience with the children within physical education, you need to see their joy and be the one who can help them take their next steps to be motivated, engaged and possibly find the next Olympians and Paralympians of the future.

Physical education lessons can have many benefits. Morgan and Hansen (2008) interviewed teachers within New South Wales, Australia, and found that teachers believed physical education to be a 'vehicle for physical activity' that 'positively impacted on learning and behaviour within the classroom' (p. 196). The Department of Education (in the UK) examined the evidence on physical education and sport in schools in 2013(b) and found that the physical benefits of physical education in childhood included 'greater bone strength and positive movement skill development' (p. 9). They also suggested that there is 'evidence that physical activity' (from physical education lessons) 'has a positive effect on the mental health in children in terms of reducing anxiety and depression and improving mood' (p. 9). The final positive benefit that was proposed by the DfE (2013b) report was that there is some evidence to indicate that physical activity is linked to improved concentration and positive behaviour in the classroom.

What does it mean to be physically educated?

According to Lounsbery and McKenzie (2015) the term 'physically educated' was defined by the 1986 National Association for Sport and Physical Education Outcomes Committee in the United States. The committee were tasked with answering the question of what is a physically educated child. Lounsbery and McKenzie (2015) report that the committee suggested that a physically educated child can 'perform a variety of physical activities; is physically fit; participates regularly in physical activity; knows the implications and benefits from involvement in physical activities and values physical activity and its contributions to a healthful lifestyle' (p. 140).

The phrase 'physical literacy' has more literature and more definitions internationally. Whitehead (2010) defined physical literacy as wherein the individual has the 'motivation, confidence, physical competence, knowledge and understanding to value and take responsibility for maintaining purposeful physical pursuits/activities throughout the lifecourse'. Whitehead (2010) proposed that this could be developed within and throughout a child's physical education lessons, not just within the primary school setting. Taking an international perspective, the Canada Sport for Life Society (2016) defines it as the cornerstone of both participation and excellence in physical activity and sport. It suggests that individuals who are physically literate are more likely to be active in life. For children to be physically literate they need to be confident in the activities they are undertaking. See also Chapter 5 and the idea of ensuring that the children are provided with clear fundamental movement skills, as building blocks for their development of physical skills which they can transfer and apply to different environments and physical activities or sports. The Pacific Institute for Sport Excellence (PISE, 2016) suggests that children should be provided with opportunities to become confident in four basic environments: on the ground, as this forms the basis for games and dance; in the water, as this forms the basis for aquatic activities; in the air, as this forms the basis for gymnastics, diving and other aerial activities. They also suggest the fourth environment – though not equally applicable within the UK except on about 3 days a year – of snow and air, as these form a basis for all winter sliding activities (PISE, 2016).

Sport Wales (2013) reported that the time before a child is 7 years old is the vital time to ensure that children are confident and become physically literate. By developing skills at a young age, within a fun and safe environment children are more likely to continue with lifelong physical activity and sport as the positive experiences enhance the children's desire to continue with activities. They highlighted that the key areas to focus on are fundamental motor skills (discussed in more detail in Chapter 5) that include stability skills, locomotor skills and object manipulation. They proposed the following equation:

Physical Skills + Confidence + Motivation + Lots of Opportunities = Physical Literacy

(Sport Wales, 2013).

Almond and Afonso (2014) suggested that care is needed when linking physical literacy to fundamental movement skills, as there are other ways to learn, for example, physical curiosity (as discussed in Chapter 5). They propose that inadequate motor skills could actually be due to insufficient opportunities in purposeful play and insufficient time to practice. As is shown within this section, there is much discussion within the literature about the terms 'physically educated' and 'physically literate'. The terms seem to be very similar and at times interchangeable. The main difference appears to be that physically educated is about doing and physically literate is about knowing. It is important for children that physical education lessons help them become both physically educated and physically literate, in that they are able to both know and do.

How can physical education contribute to a child's whole education?

Learning within physical education can help the child's whole education, as the children can learn through the domains of learning. (For early years this will be discussed in Chapter 5.) Over the years there has been much debate as to the number of domains of learning (Figure 1.12). Kirk (1993) originally proposed three domains. He identified the first as Psychomotor, which included learning and performance of

Figure 1.12 The domains of learning and how they have been applied over the years

Psychomotor	Affective	Cognitive

Kirk's 1993 Domains of Learning

Psychomotor	Affective	Cognitive	Social

Laker's 2000 Domains of Learning

Practical	Cognitive	Social

Howells' 2015 Application of the Domains of Learning to the National Curriculum and Early Years Foundation

Stage.

skills and practice activities such as fitness and coordination. Affective was the second domain and included intra-personal skills, positive attitudes, health awareness, good self-esteem, values and motivation. The third domain was the cognitive domain and included knowledge and understanding, the ability to make decisions, to plan, to evaluate and to think creatively. Laker (2000) developed Kirk's original domains further and introduced the social domain, which included interpersonal skills, pro-social behaviour, team membership, group work and leadership. Howells (2015) has applied these domains of learning to reflect the new National Curriculum and the Early Years Foundation Stage (see Chapter 5). These domains included Practical, which focuses on the physical aspects of learning; Cognitive, which includes links to vocabulary, problem solving, overcoming challenges, and expressing feelings; and the final domain of Social, which includes collaboration and communicating and coping in particular with losing or not winning (Figure 1.12).

With children not just learning 'sports' but actually applying what they are learning to domains, their ways of learning within other subjects can be improved and developed. However, it is up to you to emphasize within the physical education lessons and physical development sessions the links to the domains of learning. For example, when playing hockey, the children need to understand not just that they are actually focusing on the physical movements of hockey, but that this can be further broken down into running and coordination and control of the stick and ball and stick (practical domain) and that they are applying and developing skills to link and make actions and sequences, which is again running with the ball and stick under control (cognitive domain). An action such as running with the ball and stick under control is both practical and cognitive learning. Plus, alongside both of these, the child is also communicating with others within their team (social domain). You need to make these links throughout the lesson and also the plenary can be useful to highlight this again to reinforce the knowledge and understanding of the learning within the lesson. Adding the domains of learning into your plans can help extend and support understanding and learning that is occurring within physical education lessons. Once you get into the habit of adding this information to lesson plans it can become much easier to see and reflect upon.

Summary

This chapter outlined and introduced you to the three areas that teachers and practitioners need to understand; physical education; physical development and physical activity. The chapter offered suggestions for how these areas could be developed through opportunities within structured and unstructured settings and also shared what is sustained physical activity and how you can support this within the school setting. The chapter highlighted the importance of understanding how a child can be physically educated as well as becoming physically literate. The chapter also explored the need for you to be part of the children's learning within physical education and to understand it from a domains of learning perspective rather than just a simple physical element. The chapter discussed how exciting the new National Curriculum for physical education (in England) is, with the emphasis on a number of 'Cs' throughout the child's journey through early years and through primary. Overall the chapter has drawn on literature to show how important physical education lessons are and how the child can be supported within physical development and physical activity. Chapter 2 will continue the theme of physical education with a focus on current developments and how competition can be used with physical education.

Recommended reading

The following three texts are provided as follow-on reading:

1   Howells, K. (2015). 'Physical Education Planning'. In K. Sewell (ed.), *Planning the Primary National Curriculum: A Complete Guide for Trainees and Teachers*. Sage: London (pp. 262–76).

2   Driscoll, P., Lambirth, A. and Roden, J. (eds) (2015). *The Primary Curriculum: A Creative Approach*, 2nd edn. Sage: London, pp. 137–55.

3   Doherty, J. and Brennan, P. (2007). *Physical Education and Development 3–11 a Guide for Teachers*. Abingdon and Oxen: Routledge and Taylor & Francis Group.

Chapter 2
Current Developments in Physical Education

Chapter objectives

- The delivery of fundamental movement skills in Key Stage 1 (children aged 4–7) and modified sports in Key Stage 2 (children aged 7–11)
- The increased importance of physical activity and physical education for health
- The use of leadership and peer-coaching strategies to develop a more holistic approach to learning in physical education
- The effective use of competition in primary school physical education to raise standards and the impact of teachers positively contributing to children's enjoyment of competition.

Introduction

This chapter will examine the current developments in physical education and it will unpack how these developments impact children's learning within physical education. In recent years, in the UK, £450 million has been spent on improving physical education and the All-Party Parliamentary Group (2016) suggests that this money has been used to deliver more and better sport and physical education. Physical education has taken a much more visible and prominent position within curriculum at primary schools. As much as this is a hugely positive step, the outcomes of increased investment, greater academic research and increased scrutiny from governments, academics and head teachers has uncovered a subject that is, arguably undergoing considerable pedagogical transformation in terms of what is taught (product), how it is taught (process) and who teaches it (people). (The product, process and people will be further discussed in Chapter 3.) The current developments will be considered through different lenses in order to understand the variety of factors that impact physical education.

This chapter will enable you to understand how and why these developments could be applied in your schools and settings to support learning within physical education lessons and beyond, and will help you to appreciate where you 'fit' within a changing environment and what you can do to embrace the demands of these 'new' approaches to teaching physical education.

Pause for thought – *Thinking about your setting*

What has been the most recent development within your school / setting in physical education?

How would you explain this development to the children and or their parents?

Fundamental movement skills and modified sports

In both numeracy and literacy there are clear skills that children need to acquire and steps and processes that children need to accomplish in order to progress to the next stage in developing 'mastery' within those subjects. For example, children need to learn the alphabet and basic phonics before structuring words and sentences. This will then support their reading skills and help them develop an appreciation for the rules of grammar and punctuation. Same is the case for physical education. Children need to develop the basic building blocks or 'Fundamental Movement Skills' before we expect them to master the more advanced skills required for lifelong involvement in physical activity and sport (Gallahue and Ozmun 2006). (See Chapter 5 for further exploration of fundamental movement skills and concepts.)

Physical education lessons in Key Stage 1 (aged 5–7) should focus on the building block movements of running, jumping, throwing, catching, agility, balance and coordination and generic skills in isolation first, then complexity should be increased as they achieve success, rather than focusing the traditional single sport or activity approach. Key Stage 2 lessons (aged 7–11) should consolidate these skills and allow opportunities for children to link combinations of skills and, in doing so, begin to undertake more complex sport-specific skills. For example, if an individual can combine jumping, catching, twisting and throwing they are beginning to construct the necessary skills to play basketball or netball. National governing bodies of sport have begun to embrace this philosophy of basic to complex skills and in doing so have begun to develop modified versions of the 'full' sport. These modified versions often use simplified rules, more developmentally appropriate equipment and resources as a 'stepping stone' for children to foster enjoyment and engagement with the sport without necessarily having to understand the complexities associated with full competition. Many of these simplified versions of the sports (such as Kwik Cricket, see Figure 2.1) have been in place for many years and have been hugely successful in integrating new children into the sports, helping develop basic skills and simple tactical awareness. Other relatively newer modified versions of 'full' sports such as

Figure 2.1 Modified version of cricket

Sportshall Athletics and Tri Golf (Table 2.1) have also invested heavily in developing child-friendly equipment, teaching resources and inspiring practice and competition formats to make sports that have been traditionally deemed inappropriate for primary-aged children now accessible for all ages.

The increased importance of physical activity and physical education for health

According to Armour and Harris (2013) 'the development of new Physical Education for health pedagogies is the next step to be taken in finding a valuable and valued role for Physical Education in the wider context of health' (p. 214). As highlighted in Chapter 1, physical education lessons have been seen as a place to encourage children to engage in lifestyles that are both healthy and physically active (Green 2002). Therefore, it is important to incorporate health pedagogies within physical education lessons. If the child's experience of physical education is anything less than 'irresistible', then teachers are failing to grasp the opportunity to make a significant difference to the children's long-term physical development, health and well-being.

At a time when increased sedentary lifestyles have been directly linked with increases in obesity levels, type 2 diabetes, cardiovascular disease and psychological ill-health (World Health Organization 2010), perhaps it is not surprising that

Table 2.1 Examples of modified sports played in primary schools (Youth Sport Trust, 2013)

Traditional sport	Modified version for KS2	Main features/differences
Athletics	Sportshall Athletics	• Indoor team format • Team relays and modified 'field' events • Modified equipment/events: for example, foam javelins, standing long jump, vertical jump, obstacle relays
Cricket	Kwik Cricket	• 8 v 8 Games • Players bat in pairs and bat for two overs • Every person balls, rotates positions • Plastic bats and stumps, use of a softer 'wind' ball • Amended scoring system so players lose runs if 'out' but stay in batting position for the whole two overs
Golf	Tri Golf	• Ten-player 'team' competition • Station-based activities or 'holes' • Adapted 'putters' and 'chippers'; (plastic, lighter, larger head) • Foam/Velcro balls
Hockey	Quicksticks	• 4 v 4 games, mixed gender • Bigger, lighter ball • Smaller, lower goals; no goalkeepers
Netball	High-5 Netball	• 5 v 5 games • No wing-defence or wing attack • Compulsory positional rotations
Rugby	Kids First (Tag) Rugby	• 4 v 4 or 6 v 6 formats (based on ability) • Non-contact • Use of tag belts and tags to 'tackle' • No scrums, lineouts, kicking
Tennis	Mini-Tennis (Red)	• Short tennis courts/nets • Low compression 'red' or foam balls • Small, short handled rackets • Simple rally scoring (1-0, 1-1 etc.)
Volleyball	VolleySport	• 2 v 2 format • Played over a badminton net • Use of 'soft touch' volleyball or beach balls

policy makers are increasingly seeing physical education lessons as an instrument to help introduce strategies to encourage lifestyle changes. Encouraging lifelong engagement in physical activity has the potential to not only save lives, but also to save governments millions of pounds spent treating illnesses in adults that could be negated through the adoption of healthier, more active lifestyles. Despite the fact that physical education lessons account for less than 2 per cent of a young person's waking time (Armour and Harris 2013), there has been a significant shift in focus in primary school physical education on the role that it plays in promoting and (where possible) delivering health benefits.

Pause for thought – *A scenario-based question:*

The Association for Physical Education (2015) recommends that children should be actively moving for 50–80 per cent of the available learning time.

How much time do you think your children are actively moving within your physical education lessons?

Physical Education is now expected to play an important role in promoting healthy lifestyles by exposing children to a wide range of physical activities in a positive and engaging manner, in the hope that it will foster engagement for activity for the rest of their lives. Many children's lives are dominated by sedentary activities, they are often isolated from their peers and statistics suggest poor diets are exasperating the impact of low activity levels. Clearly, the need for high-quality and engaging physical education lessons is paramount. The UK Government's 'Everybody Active, Every Day' report (Public Health England 2014) suggests that all children between the age of 5 and 18 should engage in a *minimum* of sixty minutes moderate-to-vigorous physical activity every day; yet only 21 per cent of boys and 19 per cent of girls aged 5–15 are actually achieving those targets. Nonetheless, Howells (2014) found a more positive result when just primary school children were considered and that it was possible for children to reach the 60-minutes target within a school day if the day included a physical education lesson, highlighting the importance of physical education in a child's life.

Listed below are some ways in which you could ensure that your children are 'physically active' for 50–80 per cent of their physical education lesson:

- Carry out logistical tasks (such as organizing groups or distributing children's responsibilities) *while* the children are getting changed
- If possible prepare as much of the working area before the lesson begins. Can a group of children or support staff lay out cones and equipment while the students are changing?
- Start the lesson with a simple activity that encourages high levels of activity from the outset with minimal instructions (such as simple 'tag' games)
- Ensure 'line drills' have no more than four children in any one line

- Set children simple individualized tasks to complete while transitioning from one activity to the next (to allow time to move cones etc.) – such as 'Count how long you can balance on your weaker foot with your eyes closed'

- Keep instructions to a minimum and give individualized support/feedback *while* the groups are performing the task

- Use a countdown from five to one when bringing the group 'in' to explain the next task/activity. (Do you *need* to bring them 'in'?)

Holistic approach to learning in physical education

National policy makers have begun to appreciate the need for schools to adopt a more holistic approach to learning in physical education. By developing strategies to increase physical activity among young people, they have been able to increase the provision of funding, resources and Continuing Professional Development (CPD) courses for schools. To support this new approach, Public Health England (PHE) (2015), working alongside key partners such as the Youth Sport Trust (YST) and the Association of Colleges Sport, produced a guidance document that outlined '8 Promising Principles for Practice' (p. 5) (see Figure 2.2) outlining the most effective strategies to encourage greater physical activity among children in schools and colleges.

Figure 2.2 '8 Promising Principles of Practice' (PHE 2015, p. 5)

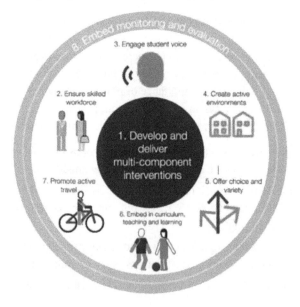

1. Deliver multi-component interventions

Conscious of the fact that there is no 'silver bullet' to get children to become more active, the report suggests that schools that adopt a whole-school/community approach are far more successful in making significant lifestyle changes. PHE (2015) recommends the creation of cross-curricular projects for teaching and learning both in the school and at home that embed the importance of physical activity through Personal Social Health and Emotion (PSHE) and across the whole curriculum. They advocate that combining school work with additional home learning strategies that teach children *and* families the benefits of adopting healthy lifestyles through fun, inspiring (and easily accessible) physical activity sessions is far more likely to have a longer-term impact on children and their families. The case study below from River School demonstrates how they involve the whole community in their 'Healthy Living' cross-curricular topic for Year 5 children. The introduction of whole-school daily physical activity initiatives such as 'Golden Mile' and 'Wake up and Shake Up' helps to build a culture for activity within the school and an ethos that transcends formal and informal learning opportunities both at school and at home. (Successful implementation of this all-encompassing 'principle' will require the effective delivery of the other seven principles.)

CASE STUDY: Using physical education to lead a cross-curricular approach to developing healthy lifestyles

Teachers at River School, Dover, developed a 'Healthy Living' cross-curricular topic for children in Year 5 that ran for half a term.

In their science lessons they discussed the impact of diet and exercise on health and well-being, exploring different food groups and discussing what a 'healthy lifestyle' meant to them. They discussed the term 'fitness' and experimented with measuring changes to their heart rates after undertaking different activities.

The children were assigned a home learning project to track their exercise levels over a three-week period and were asked to maintain a food diary for the same period. They then used their numeracy skills to create graphs and charts to plot their outcomes. Each child created a poster titled 'Healthy Living' that was displayed in the school hall.

In their weekly PE lessons the children were taken through different fitness classes: pilates, yoga, tai chi and boxercise. Where possible, qualified parents/ fitness instructors were invited to deliver these sessions, while on other occasions the group followed online fitness classes.

The class were also taken to a local leisure centre to discover the different fitness 'opportunities' available to people in the local community and had the chance to 'have a go' on treadmills, spinning bikes and cross-training machines. In small groups the children were able to interview different people at the leisure centre and used their findings to create a piece of creative writing for their literacy lessons.

For the final lesson of the term, the class invited parents and relatives to attend their physical education lesson. The children took turns to lead portions of a fitness class for the attendees, each having designed a short routine that demonstrated their knowledge of the different fitness classes they had experienced. The session finished with the children distributing glow sticks, turning out the lights and delivering a high-energy 'clubercise' routine!

If physical education lessons account for only 2 per cent of a young person's waking time (Armour and Harris, 2013), the involvement of the wider community in creating positive attitudes towards developing healthy and active lifestyles is crucial. Moreover, the involvement of parents makes the experience more engaging and pleasurable for the children. The children at River certainly loved seeing their families struggle to keep up with the fitness routines that they created and delivered!

2. Ensure a skilled workforce

PHE (2015) proposed the need to have staff who feel suitably confident and competent to create effective experiences for children that increase physical activity within lessons while also meeting the objectives of the National Curriculum for physical education. Various national providers and sports governing bodies now offer CPD opportunities for teachers specifically designed to help encourage greater physical activity in physical education lessons. For example, the Lawn Tennis Association's 'Cardio Tennis Course' or the YST's 'Start to Move' programme are designed for teachers of all abilities and provide a range of practical and online resources to use in lessons. Schools may consider using a portion of their sport premium funding (DfE 2016) to support the costs incurred with upskilling staff or using suitably qualified professionals to deliver specific activity sessions to support learning.

3. Engage student voice

Chapter 3 will discuss in more detail the importance of focusing on the 'receiver' (the children) in order to create irresistible physical education lessons. However, engaging the children and empowering them to take some ownership in the physical activity to be delivered will enhance the chances of them maintaining a higher level of engagement. This requires you to take risks (see Chapter 8) beyond your own physical education experiences, to ensure that children receive exposure to a broad range of different types of activity within lessons that go far beyond the traditional team games and sports that are delivered. (See also Principle 5.) In addition, the use of young people to act as inspirational role models (sport ambassadors) to officiate, to lead teams, to report on activities and support younger children can have a huge impact in encouraging others to adopt similar good habits and follow a similar active path (Figure 2.3).

Figure 2.3 Children acting as sports ambassadors, discussing videos they had filmed on their cameras

4. Create active environments

In order to encourage greater physical activity among children, schools need to ensure maximum use of open spaces, playgrounds and parks within the school and the local community (see also Chapter 8). Investing in loose and fixed equipment for children to use on the playground and upgrading existing facilities can positively impact activity among children (Figure 2.4). These need not be overly expensive; the report suggests that non-traditional objects such as car tyres, tunnels or milk crates can be effective in encouraging greater 'active play' throughout the school day.

5. Offer choice and variety

Schools that offer a broad and varied range of physical activity opportunities both in structured physical education lessons and during 'free play' at break or lunchtimes are more likely to see greater 'take up' from larger numbers of children. Alternative activities (Figure 2.5) that place greater emphasis on participation, focusing on fun rather than competition, may encourage greater involvement from those children who are less engaged (and consequently likely to be more inactive) when taking part in more traditional sports. Traditional playground games and activities such as hopscotch and skipping have been popular for many years, after all, and are still popular today.

Figure 2.4 Benjamin exiting a tunnel at sports day

Figure 2.5 Riley enjoying using the fixed equipment, designed to encourage active play and to challenge the children in jumping, balance, agility and coordination skills

6. Embed in curriculum, teaching and learning

The National Curriculum for physical education in England (DfE 2013) aims to ensure that all children are 'physically active for sustained periods of time'. Moreover, lessons should provide opportunities for children to become physically 'competent and confident' in a manner that will enable them to develop the skills to

Figure 2.6 Children answering a numeracy question, forming the number 17 using their bodies

sustain lifelong physical activity. Beyond physical education lessons, however, you could also encourage movement and activity within other lessons to avoid sedentary behaviours. For example, in numeracy lessons why not ask the children to work in groups of two or three to answer simple arithmetic questions by using their bodies to create the shape of the correct answer? (Figure 2.6)

Pause for thought – *An activity for trial*:

Can you think of examples of where you could introduce an element of physical activity into your classroom-based lessons each day? Over the course of the week add these into your lesson plans and have a go at these in non-physical education lessons.

What skills have you found at the end of the week that can be transferred from physical education to your other subjects? This addition of activities could add significantly to a child's activity level.

---

7. Promote active travel

Many schools already embrace active travel initiatives to encourage children to walk at least part of the way to school on one or more days a week. Creating a 'Walking Bus' or 'Park and Stride' scheme helps to increase activity levels in a manner that also helps encourage wider community engagement in physical activity. Schools that offer more provisions for children to cycle or scooter to school (through the creation of scooter sheds, for example) are also more likely to see greater 'buy in' from parents and children to such schemes. Schools have used sport premium funding (DfE 2016) to pay for a fitness instructor to deliver a thirty-minute fitness session on the playground for parents and carers at 9.00 am on the day they encouraged families to walk to school. Other schools have had active transport competitions to encourage all within the classes to walk/scooter/cycle in.

8. Embed monitoring and evaluation

Projects that encourage self-monitoring have been found to support an increase in physical activity over sustained periods of time, particularly among the less active children. Be it via children keeping activity diaries or the use of pedometers or activity-tracking apps on phones and tablets, collecting physical activity data also provides opportunities for cross-curricular learning in numeracy lessons. Schools that collect data may also be able to use it as evidence of the 'impact' of physical activity initiatives, which may be beneficial in securing additional funding opportunities in the future.

The effective use of competition in primary school physical education

The effective use of competition within physical education lessons and school sport has been the source of much discussion for many years (particularly with regard to where it 'fits' in primary school education). Parents, head teachers, researchers and policy makers often share opposing perspectives, usually based upon personal philosophies that reflect individual experiences of competition in sport that they had themselves either as participants or spectators. On the one hand, competition can be seen as an effective tool to help develop skills, encourage physical activity, build character, appreciate and respect others, and prepare children for the 'real life' (Bernstein et al. 2011; Shields and Funk 2011). On the other hand, competition is also seen as encouraging the polar opposite in many; it is perceived as benefitting only the more able performers; competition diminishes self-esteem, excludes students from achieving success, reduces participation and even promotes cheating, aggression and violence (Kohn 1986; Shields and Bredemeier 2011). Laker (2000) suggested that physical education lessons were the ideal setting for allowing children to explore how to cope with winning and losing to develop sporting behaviours. Yet, Richardson (2011) found that two-thirds of children aged 8–16 reacted badly when they lost and their parents also behaved badly when watching their children lose! This highlights how important emotional development (in the social domain) is, alongside competition, for our young children.

Ofsted, taking inspiration from the recent success of Team GB at London 2012 Games, visited ten independent schools, thirty-five state schools and collected the views of over five hundred head teachers and thousand young people to explore the impact of competitive school sport. Their findings pointed to a direct positive correlation between schools that offer high-quality competitive sporting opportunities and wider achievement in academic subjects (Ofsted 2014). Within the publication 'Going the extra mile; excellence in competitive sport' Chief Inspector Sir Michael Wilshaw claims that 'schools that win on the field win in the exam hall' (p. 3).

How does this translate into effective teaching of physical education in primary schools? How should you seek to introduce competition within your lessons without fostering some of the negative and less favourable outcomes that were highlighted above? This section will firstly seek to define what is meant by the term competition, suggesting that many of the negative misconceptions related to competition evolve from misunderstanding what competition actually *is*. Next, we will explore why competition *is* a valuable pedagogical tool by exploring the impact that it can have across each of the 'domains of learning' that Howells (2015) applied to the physical education National Curriculum. Helping you to appreciate different 'types' of competition can assist them in designing appropriate tasks to challenge different groups of children; as such, three simple classifications of competition within physical education lessons will be discussed for individuals, pairs and teams of all ages. Finally, a simple model for effective competition will be introduced to demonstrate when true competition is *most effectively* employed and where; conversely, poorly delivered competition has the potential for lowering self-esteem, fostering poor effort and application from children.

Competition to raise standards in physical education and school sport

Defining competition

'Rather than assume students understand competition it is vital that they are educated about it.'

TRUE COMPETITION *'Striving WITH'*
A healthy desire to excel

- A process in which participants seek excellence by trying to surmount the challenge provided by an opponent
- Enjoyment is found in the strenuous pursuit of worthy goals
- Competition serves the mutual interest of all participants
- It is based upon a 'contest-as-partnership' understanding

DECOMPETITION *'Striving AGAINST'*
An unhealthy desire merely to beat the opponent

- A process in which participants seek to demonstrate superiority over opponents
- Enjoyment is found in the extrinsic rewards that come at the expense of others
- Decompetition serves only the interest of the victor
- It is based upon a 'contest-as-war' understanding

(Shields and Funk 2011, p. 9)

Leading up to and beyond the London 2012 Olympic and Paralympic Games, the government at the time took a stance towards promoting competitive sports within physical education and school sport in an attempt to create an Olympic legacy within the country, through the development of education programmes such as 'Get Set' and 'School Games'. However, within physical education it is often the first time children will encounter any sort of formal sporting competition and therefore it is important not to 'put children off'. If, as the National Curriculum suggests, competitive experiences 'build character and help to embed values such as fairness and respect' (DfE 2013, p. 155), it is first crucially important that children understand the true definition of competition (see box above). The word itself evolves from the Latin word *competre* – meaning 'to strive *with*'. It is often misunderstood, however, as meaning often virtually the opposite; the need to achieve success by striving *against* others (Shields and Funk 2011).

Examples of 'striving with'

A recent meme circulating social media showed two athletes playing 'head tennis' (a mix of football and table tennis) across a table tennis table. In a spectacular exhibition of skill and agility the two performers produced an incredible rally whereby the ball (the size of a handball) was sent back and forth across the table, using only headers, with each header pushing the 'opponent' to reach further, attempting even more complex movements and stretching themselves to their physical limits. Neither player would have achieved the same level of performance had their 'opponent' not displayed an equally high level of determination and technical aptitude. The performance of one athlete simply caused the other to 'raise their game' in a spectacular fashion, with sublime results; it was the level of performance of each performer that drove improvements in the other.

Similarly, another video clip showed two teams of canoeists sitting facing each other at opposing ends of the *same* boat attempting a 'tug of war'. Despite each canoeist paddling frantically, the canoe did not budge an inch. The harder one team paddled, the more the opposing team at the other end of the boat battled against them. Again, it was the nature of the competition, the two teams 'striving' with each other, that drove the increased effort from all participants. In the two examples listed above, neither of the head tennis players would have pushed themselves physically and emotionally or (arguably) gained as much pleasure from the sense of achievement from their 'performance' had they not been so equally matched in their contest. Likewise, neither group of canoeists would have benefitted from the scenario if one team simply overpowered the other within seconds of the 'contest' taking place.

Shields and Bredemeier (2009) define this approach as '**true competition**'; competition taking place where one person or team strives to raise their performance (and seek excellence) in trying to overcome the challenge set by others. It is the *process* rather than the *outcome* that raises performance; enjoyment comes from the strenuous pursuit of worthwhile goals. 'It is the exhilaration, excitement, and sense of accomplishment that comes with maximising one's physical and mental potential in the pursuit of a goal' (Shields and Funk 2011, p. 8).

By contrast, where individuals or teams are motivated only by the *outcomes,* rather than the *process,* where the focus is more on 'winning' and achieving superiority over others, then '**decompetition**' is evident. Often driven by extrinsic rewards, goals shift from achieving excellence to simply reaching conquest over others, regardless of how it is achieved. In these situations, only the interest of the victors is served and in doing so they will often look to 'win' as quickly as possible, even if that means humiliating the opponent, 'bending' rules and overly celebrating what they perceive as success. Failure to 'win' makes their performance worthless, with nothing achieved. Furthermore, they will often seek to appoint 'blame' by criticizing others, questioning officials, and eventually losing interest all together because of low self-esteem and sense of self-worth. This tendency to 'blame' or to explain achievement as simply being 'luck' occurs because the process has not been understood, and this can often happen in primary school if the focus for the young children is just on the outcome. You need to be confident in examining tactics and then further developing the understanding of attacking and defending processes within competition (DfE 2013). For our very young children, the simple notion of moving towards the right goal and understanding the correct direction of play may be the first skills to accomplish in a team competition setting, rather than simply focusing on scoring more goals than the other team.

For children there is often the misconception that the pleasure in competing comes simply from 'winning'. These perceptions of how children view competition are often driven by influential others (parents, coaches, peers) and misguided expectations placed upon them. It is not competition per se that is the issue, but the interpretation of what true competition actually is, and it is your role to set appropriate challenges while clearly defining what the desired outcomes of competition actually are. If used effectively and appropriately, as a tool to challenge children to focus their attention and refine their skills, then competition becomes a valuable instrument for personal development. When you use competition effectively it can have the same impact as other recognized pedagogical approaches, such as the use differentiation, adopting different teaching styles and the effective use of observation, assessment and feedback in helping individuals achieve their true potential.

The effective use of competition to raise standards in physical education and school sport

Competition and domains of learning

The question for us, however, remains: How can competition support learning in primary physical education lessons? Chapter 1 explained how Physical Education

Table 2.2 Competition identified in Howells' 2015 application of the domains of learning

Practical	Cognitive	Social
• Skills are often best learnt initially in isolation or 'closed' environments. Competition allows for these learned skills to be developed within increasingly 'open' (or changing) environments, via passive and gradually fully opposed situations	• Effective decision making can be crucial to success	• Mixed groupings to allow all to be more successful, such as less able children working with more able to achieve
• Competition allows children to perform skills in context where there is real value and meaning to the correct execution of learned skills	• Goal-oriented targets and focus gives greater need for correct decisions and tactics to achieve goals.	• Fun from working collaboratively together on focused and shared goals
• Competitive environments have been proven to sharpen children's focus and attention –it naturally inspires many to try harder to 'surmount the challenge posed by others'	• Understand need for tactics, and when to apply tactics	• Appreciation of feelings from winning and losing
• The need to adhere to rules and protocols becomes apparent in competitive environments, thus encouraging children to refine their technique – ensuring that a long jump take-off is 'behind the line' or that the distance is measured from the correct landing point, for example	• Effective for understanding and evaluating own performance and that of others (see Chapter 7 for assessment in physical education)	• Chances to do, review and evaluate through debriefing and refining future 'tactics'
		• Appreciation of value of different roles or functions others may perform, for example leader, assister and how valuable the person is who assists in the movement of play

can support a child's 'whole education' as children can learn through the different domains of learning. Howells (2015) applied these domains of learning to the National Curriculum and Table 2.2 now applies competition to the same domains, suggesting how competition can be used to support the learning that takes place in physical education lessons.

Methods of competition

Table 2.2 adapts work by Skultety (2011) to define three different *types* of competition that you may wish to employ within lessons, each with their own unique learning opportunities and educational benefits but also requiring some consideration of when and where they may be most appropriately used. Another way of reflecting on the different ways competition is used to enhance performance in physical education is to look at *how* it is delivered. Competition requires an individual to work hard to accomplish a *personal* goal; hence competing against themselves removes the possible negative implications of them being outperformed by others. There are, however, equal benefits from competing in pairs or as part of a larger team.

Individual – personal bests

When working with younger children the most effective way to introduce a level of competition is through the creation of simple, individualized challenges, or 'personal bests'. Children can work at their own level and pace to achieve the sense of success by overcoming simple measureable targets. Those targets may simply be the challenge of 'beating' a previous attempt or score, or a goal they set for themselves, based upon their own perception of their level of ability. (This in itself links with other areas of the curriculum, such as numeracy, whereby the ability to accurately predict or estimate an outcome is a measure of the individual's awareness of the subject content, or, in this case, their own physical ability.) This approach 'protects' younger children from some of the self-esteem issues that may arise from feeling inadequate or inferior to their peers, as the competition in this environment is entirely with themselves. However, some of the positives and benefits that arise from competition – a sense of achievement, the ability to reflect upon and analyse performance as a means to develop improvement and the need to 'fairly' adhere to set rules and protocols – can all be experienced in this process.

Pairs – cooperatively, collaboratively and competitively

Partner working provides many different opportunities for you to create elements of competition in a fun and challenging manner. The way pairs are created and interact can vary depending on how the 'competition' is delivered. Partners can either work cooperatively, collaboratively or competitively:

Cooperatively – This model works with one partner acting as the coach for the other who adopts the role of performer. Peer-coaching opportunities enable individuals to work alongside a partner to provide both support and encouragement, and also the chance to observe and give feedback on how performances can be improved. Similar to 'personal bests', the competition is provided by the need for a child to achieve individual goals, but on this occasion they have a 'partner' to help coach them. In these environments pairs can be of mixed ability; friends often work well together, particularly the first time they attempt this approach, as it requires individuals to have confidence to communicate effectively with each other.

Figure 2.7 Collaborative competition in New Age Kurling

Collaboratively – This format describes partners working together towards a *shared* goal or target. Competing alongside others, it could be in the format of a simple relay whereby one child goes first, followed by their partner. Alternatively, when competing against others it may be a 2 v 2 game with the two individuals forming a very simple team. As shown in the Figure 2.7, children are engaged in a 2 v 2 game of New Age Kurling, where the children are working together within their team to tactically beat the other team.

Competitively – In these activities partners directly compete against each other. Although this approach naturally creates winners and losers, you could encourage children to respect and appreciate the performance of each other. For instance, the pair can use the opportunity not only to explore *how* one individual was able to outperform the other to make an improvement in the practical domain, but also to discuss how each one 'feels' as a winner and loser in order to develop skills in the social domains.

Teams

Traditional views of competition often relate to images of one team gaining superiority over another and the subsequent positive and negative connotations of the emotional fallout from such occasions. However, when trying to use competition to enhance performance, teams can be used in very different ways beyond these very traditional games-based approaches that can be guilty of focusing simply on winning and losing.

Overload – Competition among groups or teams does not always require evenly numbered or equal ability teams. The game of 'piggy in the middle' is a simple example of where the principle of 'overload' can be applied to help develop particular skills in competitive environments. Giving a clear advantage to one team encourages that team to exploit the advantages they have. A 4 v 2 'piggy in the middle' throwing and catching game encourages (and directly rewards) those individuals who find open spaces, thus creating valuable teaching and learning opportunities. (See Figure 2.8.)

Team building and problem-solving – Competing in teams allows children to develop important social skills: the ability to work effectively with others, the importance of listening as well as talking, following as well as leading others. Team-building challenges and problem-solving tasks are designed to develop these social skills and attributes. Most often, those teams who are able to work effectively together are more likely to be more successful in completing the challenges. In these situations, the 'competition' comes from the challenge or problem rather than directly from another team or opponent. Indeed, to help children focus on developing their social and problem-solving skills it is often more effective to remove the distraction of opposing teams by setting *different* tasks for different teams and allowing them to complete them on a carousel basis. Figure 2.9 shows an example of a team-building challenge that has been set to get the whole team over

Figure 2.8 Competition overload (child with back to the camera has the ball in his hands)

Figure 2.9 Team-building competition

the 'cobweb' and to the other side. They have to work together to help each other up and over to the other side.

Differing roles and responsibilities – When children work together in competitive team situations they learn very quickly the important role that each individual can play in achieving 'team' success. Appreciation of individual strengths and the roles that different individuals perform can also help you to introduce different positions and playing formations, whereby they can openly discuss (cognitively) what each performer's role is and who may best possess the relevant qualities to fill each role. The Sport Education Model (Siedentop 1994) (discussed in further detail in Chapter 3) goes one step further, teaching children a greater appreciation

Figure 2.10 Children's coaching manual

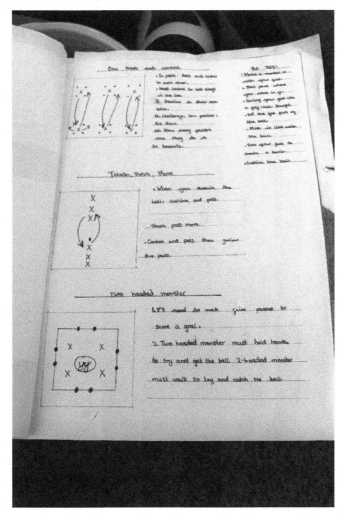

of sporting competition in its fullest sense; the model encourages children to work in teams in which individuals have extended responsibilities beyond simply being players. This enables them to learn the role of the coach, officials, event coordinators, trainers and statisticians and means that teams that succeed in sport education do not rely purely on those who are effective in the practical domain. The 'less sporty' children can make as equally valuable a contribution to their 'team' as their sporty counterparts by making use of their strengths in other areas. Figure 2.10 illustrates a coaching manual developed for use as a coach within sport education.

The following table (Table 2.3) shows the different types of competition and where and when to effectively use them.

Table 2.3 Different types of competition and where and when to effectively use them

Type of competition	Examples	Learning opportunities	Considerations for teachers
Competing Against Others Traditional sporting competition; one individual/team tries to outwit the other, while the other looks to hinder their progress. *The competition is directly posed by the opponent(s) performance and score.*	'Modified Games'; tag rugby, high 5 netball, mini-tennis, Quicksticks hockey	• Developing tactical awareness • Understanding differences in attacking and defending • Appreciation of different roles or positions • Fair play and sportsmanship	• Teams/individuals work best when evenly matched (ability) • Can you create different roles for children (officials/coaches/trainers) as per the Sports Education Model? • Competition Questioning: What can you do to …? (Strategy) • This 'type' of competition is most likely to be seen where 'decompetitive' behaviours occur • Praise and reward understanding, effort and progress rather than the score • Differentiation by people works well here (teams do not always need to be even numbers when developing tactical awareness)

Competing Alongside Others Children/teams compete to beat others by achieving the longest distance, fastest time or best score through demonstrating mastery of skills. Their performance is not directly influenced by others, but may motivate children to work harder. *The competition is to improve upon an individual's own personal best.*	Sportshall Athletics events (running, throwing, jumping) Gymnastics	• Helps individual skill mastery (FMS) • Creates peer-coaching opportunities, introduces methods for measuring and scoring (numeracy) • Develops estimating skills (how far/how many do you think you can achieve?) • Teaches the appreciation of quality, control and efficiency of movement	• Creation of pairs/groups who work well together • Reward personal improvement (measurable and aesthetic) • Great opportunities for children to create their own goals and targets • Competition questioning: How far/fast/many/long/good (mastery) • To avoid direct comparisons children can rotate around 'stations' performing different activities at each station • Differentiation by equipment works well here
Competing with Others Children work in pairs or in teams to overcome challenges. Team-building and problem-solving activities are examples of when groups compete together. *The competition is to overcome the task rather than to beat other children to it.*	Team-building and problem-solving activities Dance (choreography)	• Encourages good communication and leadership skills • Enquiry/problem-solving challenges • Rewards innovation and creativity	• Groups should be completely mixed. Different children often 'shine' in these formats • Reward initiative, innovation and creativity • The ability to debrief/reflect becomes very important here • Beware of 'social loafers' (Slavin 1995); those who sit back and rely on others • Competition questioning: How can you … (Problem-solving/reflection) • Differentiation by task works well here

How can you positively contribute to children's enjoyment of competition within physical education?

Competition and an increase in physical activity

Increased media exposure has seen significant developments in dance as a competitive activity, with many families tuning in weekly during the winter period to see celebrities compete in different dance genres in *Strictly Come Dancing*, for example. This increased exposure, as Howells (2014) reported, can increase physical activity levels and help inspire more children to undertake competitive activities. Sometimes the more individual areas such as dance, gymnastics, swimming and athletics are forgotten. Yet, these are often the easiest to measure in terms of performance as scores can apply to clear objective measurements (Howells 2015), such as distance and time. In gymnastics/dance set criteria can be applied to the evaluation and analysis of the performance. Using such elements can also help young children continue to be involved in competition outside of physical education lessons.

Pause for thought – *Thinking about what you currently do:*

How do you currently positively praise your children in physical education? How many times do you think you do this within one lesson?

In a lesson that includes a competitive activity, either observe a colleague or be brave and ask a colleague to record the number of times you use feedback about how to improve or whether you just use praise by itself and house points. Compare what you thought you did to what your colleague observed.

Shields and Bredemeier (2009, p. 44) proposed that the thought of winning and the idea of achieving is the 'driving force' which creates a competitive partnership with players, individuals, both on and off the team. The idea of winning can become a motivating aspect for children due to the intrinsic and extrinsic rewards that come with it. Most children will thrive from a reward whether it is from a person praising them on how they are doing or with the use of a trophy representing winning or for other excellence (Figure 2.11). However, Burton and Raedeke (2008) found that the use of rewards can actually make or break a child's motivation towards sport if they do not achieve and do not receive praise. Therefore, there is a need to know how you are positively contributing to the children's enjoyment of competition. This could be done, through considering your use of house points, medals and positive praise;

Figure 2.11 Sam and Samuel celebrating

do the children understand why they are getting the reward? It is key for children to understand why they have achieved such a reward; can the children describe and use movement vocabulary to analyse their performance and evaluate their success as per the National Curriculum (DfE 2013)? Try to use movement words when you are describing why something worked, why something was fantastic, why that tactic did or did not work, so the children can repeat and continue to want to undertake physical activity and sport beyond physical education lessons.

A model for effective learning in competition

The most effective competitive environments occur when the challenge posed by the task or opponent is such that the individuals have the ability to 'succeed' (rather than necessarily 'win') but are required to work hard and apply themselves in order to achieve that success. A simple model to demonstrate the interwoven relationships between challenge, success, child effort and their self-esteem is shown

Figure 2.12 Competition learning zone

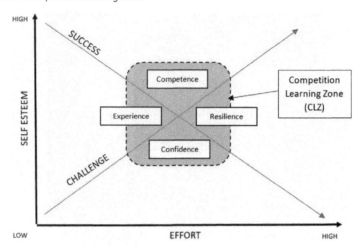

*Please note that there are, of course, some benefits to be gained from competition in areas beyond the CLZ. For example, when a team performs heroic acts of 'giant killing' (i.e. beating a team considered vastly superior to them) it can have an incredible impact on their self-esteem. However, within a teaching environment, if challenges were consistently set that were way above and beyond children's perceived level of ability, motivation and effort would soon drop if they failed to achieve at least some success on a more consistent basis.

above, whereby the competition learning zone (CLZ) is where the most consistently effective 'competition for learning' takes place.*

When the level of competition is such that individuals or teams achieve success with limited effort or whereby the challenge posed by the task or opponents does not 'stretch' the children, there is limited 'competition learning'. From a practical teaching perspective, this often leads to the more able performers becoming quickly distracted from the task as they seek to be challenged or engaged by other means. Equally, when the challenge posed by the competition is such that it is beyond the realistic ability of the individual or team to achieve any success, then the 'competition' has little value for the performer; failure to achieve some perceived level of success can quickly impact their motivation to try and therefore the effort they apply to the task. When children perceive that they cannot succeed, they often 'give up' and stop trying.

The role of the teacher is to ensure that whenever you create competitive environments within your lessons you 'pitch' it in such a way that some level of *success* is obtainable by all children, provided they apply themselves, they push themselves and make the *effort* to reach goals and targets posed by the challenge of opponents or tasks. When working in the CLZ, success provides positive *experiences* whereby hard work and effort is rewarded by increased *competence* and *confidence*. Furthermore, this fosters greater determination and *resilience* when tasks or opponents become more challenging; when success becomes harder to achieve.

Summary

The report published in 2016 by an All-Party parliament group on a 'Fit and healthy Childhood' made headlines when it declared that for far too long physical education had been considered the 'Cinderella subject' in UK schools. Calling for radical changes in the way the subject is perceived and delivered the report makes a range of recommendations, including

- increasing the number of specialist primary physical education teachers in primary schools
- having a designated physical activity coordinator in every early years setting
- creating teams in every school dedicated to promoting all types of physical activity
- all schools examining how they can improve the physical education experience for disabled children
- embedding physical education into all teacher training programmes

This chapter has sought to explore how much of the evolution (or perhaps revolution) proposed by this report has already begun, directly impacting how physical education is taught at primary schools. There is some irony in the fact that much of the 'shift' has been driven by external factors that, arguably, are polar opposites. The push for greater levels of physical activity within lessons and the need for 'health for Physical Education pedagogies' (Armour and Harris 2013) has encouraged increased investment and support to address the growing challenges of child obesity and increasingly sedentary lifestyles. Different approaches have been discussed here outlining strategies that you can employ to address these challenges, both within physical education lessons and through the development of more holistic strategies to improve physical activity across the whole curriculum, embracing the wider school and home community as part of the process.

At the other end of the scale, Ofsted's review of where Team GBs recent sporting success originated, coupled with research that suggests a direct correlation between schools that have outstanding physical education and school sport programmes and high academic achievement, has raised the profile of competition as an effective tool to enhance performance within physical education. The definition of 'true competition' (as opposed to 'decompetition') has been explained alongside greater clarification of the types of competition that can be used in lessons. Finally, a model explaining where and when competition is most effective has been suggested, highlighting the CLZ where you could aspire to deliver your competitive practices. The next chapter will take into consideration the current developments within the subject outlined in this chapter by exploring how you can make physical education a truly 'irresistible' subject for all.

Recommended reading

The following three texts are provided as follow-on reading:

1   Armour, K. and Harris, J. (2013). Making the Case for Developing New PE-for-Health Pedagogies. *Quest,* 65(2), 201–19.

2   Shields, D. L. and Funk, C. (2011). Teach to Compete. *Strategies: A Journal for Physical and Sport Educators*, 24(5), 8–11.

3   Skultety, S. (2011). Categories of Competition. *Sport, Ethics and Philosophy,* 5(4), 433–46.

Chapter 3
Physical Education as an Irresistible Activity

Chapter objectives

- Why should physical education be an irresistible activity?
- What does 'irresistible' physical education look like?
- How you can make PE irresistible for all?
  - ○ The new model for interaction and engagement – Sender, Receiver, Outcome (SRO)
  - ○ Positive modelling behaviours
  - ○ Effective ways to make physical education irresistible
- How you can positively engage and encourage *all* children within physical education?
- Why is physical education so important and why now, more than ever, it is imperative to make the subject 'irresistible' for all?

Introduction

This chapter will explore how physical education can be an irresistible activity, both for you teaching the subject and the participating children. As highlighted in Chapter 2, current developments have increased the focus and importance of physical education within the primary setting. Through the use of a brand new interaction and engagement model, the chapter will help guide you through different approaches to deliver highly active and stimulating lessons. The chapter will also consider challenges of working with children of diverse abilities, along with simple practical examples to help organize and facilitate differentiated lessons that challenge and engage all.

Why should physical education be irresistible?

Physical education offers far more to children than simply the opportunity to learn how to move effectively and efficiently in a series of different practical situations (AfPE 2008). It is a really exciting subject as it can develop enquiry and reasoning skills, encourage creativity and problem-solving; provide opportunities for children to develop social and cooperative skills; apply moral and aesthetic judgements; and develop astute tactical awareness of how and when to apply the most appropriate physical actions.

The aspirational outcome of an irresistible physical education programme is for children to be physically literate, which, Whitehead (2010) implied, would be responsible for the development of a lifelong passion for, and engagement with, physical activity and sport. By this definition, physical education demands a great deal more from you than simply teaching the skills and rules of different sports. Yet, for many years physical education has been criticized for being too traditionally game oriented, focusing more on the development of elite performers and taught in a very teacher-led, didactic style that does not engage all children (Raymond 1998). Teachers have been more concerned with the 'product' of physical education than the 'process' or modes of delivery. This was highlighted by Cale and Harris (2011, p. 57), who suggested that teachers often preach about a 'fitness for life' philosophy, yet a 'fitness for sports performance' approach is often adopted as they look to develop the most able players for sports teams rather than foster lifestyle habits for all children.

Teaching physical education differs from teaching other subjects only in terms of the content that is delivered and the environment in which it is taught. One of the best pieces of advice to give to you if you feel like you lack the confidence and competence to teach physical education is to simply take all of the principles of 'best practice' that you apply in your classroom teaching to create a positive learning 'experience' for the children, but simply deliver them in a different environment. You work confidently towards developing literacy and numeracy in the classrooms using engaging and progressive teaching strategies. The next section will look at exploring how these 'best practices' can be developed with physical literacy as the desired outcome.

What does 'irresistible' physical education look like?

When unpacking what irresistible physical education looks like, there are three parts of the lesson that need consideration in exploring 'best practice'. These include effective 'process' (how you teach) and appropriate 'product' (what you teach), but with the 'people' (who you teach) as the central focus of every interaction. This centres on you as playing the pivotal role in being the sender of delivering effective lessons; you can do this through a combination of the acquisition of essential knowledge, the demonstration of appropriate positive modelling behaviours, and the ability to adapt methodologies to best suit the audience, the environment and desired outcomes.

The process, product and people approach can be aligned with the most recent guidelines from Ofsted in their 2013 report 'Beyond 2012 – Outstanding Physical Education for all'. The report outlines its findings and recommendations from inspections at 120 primary schools over a four-year period for outstanding physical education. For schools where they judged the teaching of physical education to be either good or outstanding, they list a number of consistent observations, which certainly fall within the three categories detailed above:

- High expectations of pupils of all abilities; pupils were inspired to achieve their best (PEOPLE)
- Excellent relationships between teachers and pupils (which often led to full engagement and high levels of enjoyment) (PEOPLE)
- Pace of learning was 'purposeful and physically active' (PRODUCT)
- Pupils had lots of opportunities to be creative, make decisions for themselves, practise and perform skills (PRODUCT)
- Lessons were 'sharply focussed' and based on high-quality long-term planning (PROCESS)
- Teachers regularly assessed pupils' work through observation and provided pertinent feedback (PROCESS)

(Ofsted 2013, pp. 15–16)

Pause for thought – *An activity to consider where your own strengths lie:*

Can you list all the elements that you feel constitute a 'highly effective' physical education lesson?

Can you place each element under one of the key categories: **people, product, process**?

Do you feel that you possess strengths in particular area(s) more than other(s)?

How can you make physical education irresistible for all?

The new model for interaction and engagement – Sender, Receiver, Outcome (SRO)

In the innovative new model of interaction and engagement, the sender, receiver, outcome (SRO) model (Figure 3.1) offers an approach to help you make physical education irresistible for all. In any interaction there is a 'Sender' of information (you) (see also Table 3.1) and a corresponding 'Receiver' of information (the children you are teaching), coupled with some desired 'Outcomes' (usually driven by the 'sender') to be (ideally) derived from the interactions. The relationship between these three factors and the priority placed upon each of them at different times can have a huge impact on the ultimate experience that the 'receiver' has.

Table 3.1 Application of being an effective sender (teacher) linked to people, product and process

Being an Effective Sender (Teacher) (Physical Education):	People	Product	Process
S sender	Understanding your audience. *'Who to teach?'*	*Subject and content knowledge.* *'What to teach?'*	Developing understanding; appropriate personality traits and effective competencies *'How to teach?'*
	• For example: • Developmental stages • Learning styles • Special educational needs • Formative and summative feedback from previous lessons • Pupil choice/preferences	• For example: • National Curriculum • Subject/topic knowledge • Schemes of work/lesson planning • Pedagogical models • School policies: • Behaviour • Assessment • Inclusion • Safety • Equipment and resources • Effective lesson planning	• For example: • Teaching styles • Communication • Positive modelling behaviours • Observation and feedback • Classroom ecology • Motivational techniques • Differentiation • Use of ICT • Cross-curricular learning • Lesson organization: pace, progress and competition

Figure 3.1 Sender, Receiver, Outcomes (SRO) model

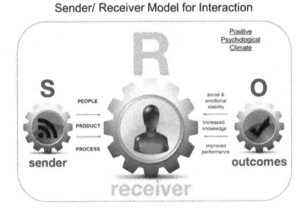

The SRO model is adapted from Russell (1989) and proposes that to achieve consistent and effective results the focus of any interaction must be the receiver. Thus, the receiver appears central to the model and larger than the other factors. To be an effective sender you need to have subject and content knowledge (PRODUCT); an understanding of the (receiver) children, their stages of development and unique learning needs (PEOPLE); and, finally the appropriate positive modelling behaviours and the ability to apply their knowledge with suitable pedagogical approaches (PROCESS) to gain the best impact; to make physical education irresistible.

Positive modelling behaviours

As you are the 'sender' in the SRO model, effective teaching in physical education starts with you. Mawer (1990) proposed that 'it's not what you do – it's the way that you do it' (p. 307) and certainly, you are responsible for setting the tone of the lesson through their positive attitude and enthusiasm. It is your ability to capture the children's imagination and to engage and maintain their interest that gives the children the confidence and reassurance to step out of their 'comfort zone'. You need to be approachable and offer support and empathy where needed, while maintaining a sense of integrity and authority via a confident and charismatic style. As much as subject knowledge and appropriate pedagogical approaches are fundamental to delivering high-quality lessons (Shulman 1987), the ability to interact and communicate with your children is 'the most single influencing factor' (Raymond 1998, p. 103).

The following positive modelling behaviours – personal appearance, body language, commitment to teach physical education, leading by example and working with specialists – are examined in more detail:

- Personal Appearance: When children area always asked to change into a suitable kit to take part in physical education lessons, it is suggested that you do likewise (Figure 3.2). You can inspire your children just by wearing a tracksuit, appropriate footwear, tying your hair back, removing non-essential jewellery as this presents the correct message to the children with regard to not only the appropriate dress code for physical activity, but also the correct attitudes and high expectations you have for the subject.

Personal appearance case study:

At White Cliffs Primary College for the Arts, not only has the school provided staff with their own kit to teach physical education, but they have also adopted a school 'identity' for their sports teams. Now teachers delivering physical education lessons and extracurricular clubs, alongside children representing the school at inter school festivals and tournaments, are doing so branded as the 'White Cliffs Hornets'.

Figure 3.2 Mr Uden in his physical education kit

- Body language: If you display a positive and enthusiastic attitude towards the subject you are more likely to receive a more positive and enthusiastic response from your children. From subtler behaviours such as simply having hands in your pockets or arms folded (Harris and Cale 2006) to displaying a reluctance to go outside in slightly inclement weather, all can be interpreted as boredom or a lack of interest in the subject.

- Commitment to teach physical education: Indeed, far too often class teachers can be guilty of indirectly devaluing the importance of physical education by not committing to delivering regular, high-quality lessons. If you are too quick to cancel physical education lessons due to the weather or because you have a facility clash with other 'important' events, such as school productions or visits, all these can devalue the subject. You wouldn't cancel numeracy to practise the nativity, so why physical education? Why not use physical education to support and explore topic areas that you're preparing for SATs, this will really show the children how much you value physical education and show them that they can learn in a variety of different ways or that physical education can help release the energy that can be built up in children. All these ideas will show children that you see physical education to be 'irresistible'.

- Leading by example: You should approach the teaching of physical education in the same way that you approach all other curriculum subjects; don't fear it, if you're worried ensure you have planned effectively. Using subject-specific schemes of work (if schools use them) can be helpful; ensure that you have clearly defined lesson objectives and outcomes for each lesson. Try to actively promote extracurricular activities at school and within the local community and, where possible, demonstrate and share your own commitment to the importance of developing a healthy and active lifestyle by becoming actively involved in after-school clubs and activity programmes. The children will love your stories of, for example, racing in the Park Run and getting a personal best or getting your wiggle on at Zumba.

- Working with specialist physical education teachers and coaches: If your school has invested in a physical education specialist or sports coaches to deliver some (or all) of their lessons, then get involved and look at them as your support agent. Physical education can be your time to develop your own subject knowledge, alongside the specialist through continuing professional development, without having to go on a course. You can also help them; you're the expert on your children and the school standards (Carney and Howells 2008) so this could materialize into a really good development time for both of you. It also provides an invaluable opportunity to observe the interactions and behaviours of the class in different environments that can assist you in providing greater individualized support across the curriculum.

Effective ways to make physical education irresistible

Pedagogical approaches in physical education have traditionally been driven by the need to enable children to 'develop competence to excel in a broad range of physical activities' (DfE 2013, p. 1). Thus, typically lessons have evolved around the need to develop skills and techniques that, once mastered, can then be applied to a range of different sports and physical activity settings. This lends itself to teaching that is teacher led in a very didactic style with children seeking to mirror demonstrations and reproduce specific movements and actions. This mode of learning can be highly effective in helping children to develop physical skills but limits creativity, self-discovery and social interaction. This approach teaches skills out of the context, and as such, children can often struggle to know (cognitively) when, where and how to apply them in a competitive or performance environment. Those children who struggle to master the basic skills (those children who may be less coordinated in a practical setting) may quickly be discouraged, particularly when they observe their peers, who seem to grasp things more quickly and, consequently, dominate competitive situations. The next sections will look at adopting different models to teaching physical education and how cross-curricular learning can be used to help make physical education lesson irresistible.

- Adopting Different Models (or Approaches) to Teaching Physical Education

Assessing children purely on their ability to perform skills effectively does have some merit in terms of analysing 'success' in physical education. However, to become physically literate requires children to also demonstrate motivation, confidence, knowledge and understanding (Whitehead 2010). This section will look at how to adopt different or alternative models that look at more holistic approaches when teaching physical education.

Many outdoor and adventurous activity (OAA) lessons can be taught using the Cooperative Learning Pedagogical Model (Slavin 1995), whereby children are encouraged to develop team building, communication and leadership skills (social domain) through problem-solving and collaborative activities. In these lessons there is limited emphasis placed on learning physical skills, but that does not mean that children are not physically active. Through the activities the children can learn valuable skills: in how to listen effectively; how to give and receive feedback; how to encourage others positively; how to plan before and evaluate after performing; as well as developing the confidence to lead others and communicate effectively within group situations. These are many of the qualities and skills that can be found wanting in some of our more able performers, allowing others to excel, boosting their self-esteem, and, hopefully their perception of physical education.

Equally, the Teaching Games for Understanding (TGFU) model (Bunker and Thorpe 1982) encourages children to develop their cognitive skills by focusing on their ability to develop and apply tactics within game situations. This places learning

Figure 3.3 Benjamin taking on the role of coach in sport education

in the context of the physical game itself; developing the correct techniques comes later as the children learn when and where they are needed. This approach is often very popular with children; after all, it addresses those players who constantly plea 'when can we play a game?'

The Sport Education Model of instruction (Siedentop 1994) was created to help children develop more authentic and enjoyable sport experiences than those typically seen in traditional physical education lessons. The children participate as members of teams throughout the unit of work, which culminates in a final festival event in the last week of the 'season'. Children take an active role in their own sport experience by serving in varied and realistic roles that we see in authentic sport settings such as coaches, trainers, statisticians, officials and publicists. Teams develop camaraderie through shared uniforms, names and cheers as they work together to learn and develop skill and tactical play. This approach allows children with different strengths the opportunity to make greater positive contributions to the team beyond merely their playing ability (Figure 3.3).

CASE STUDY: Using the Sport Education Model to teach football at River Primary School, Dover (See sample lesson plan at end of chapter and Figure 3.3.)

Class teachers had become very frustrated teaching football to Year 6 children (age 10 – 11 years) with lessons dominated by the more able children whose technical ability often dwarfed that of the teachers and whose reluctance to take on-board instruction and overly competitive behaviour often disrupted the quality of learning for the rest of the class.

At River, the teacher ensured that members of the school football team became coaches and were required to devise and deliver short coaching sessions for their 'team' each week. Children with experience in other sports were invited to become team trainers and were responsible for leading their team's warm-up and cool-down sessions, while other members of the class became match officials, score keepers and equipment coordinators; each selected based upon their abilities and preferences.

This approach to teaching physical education may have achieved less in enhancing the children's football playing abilities. However, the children were able to develop other vital skills and appreciate values such as the rules, rituals, traditions and the sense of belonging and camaraderie that comes from being part of an effective team when playing sports. These are all qualities that may not typically be developed in traditional skills and games-focused physical education lessons.

Both children and teachers clearly took a great deal from the experience:

'It's really hard to find the words to describe how much I enjoyed it and I want to do it again. It was such a great experience to show me that sport isn't all about winning. (And I used to hate PE and Games.)' **Year 6 (previously reluctant) child**

Watching this approach to teaching Physical Education was as much an eye-opening experience as it was a pleasure.. What struck me most was the powerful inclusion showed by the children who handled the delicate balance of wanting to win and allowing their peers with difficulties to get a chance at the ball. I was thrilled when one usually disaffected autistic child rose to the challenge of being a ref, demonstrating excellent learning about rules - I was even more impressed when the same child then took her turn as a player and ran after the ball. I enjoyed seeing the always sporty child realise how important it was to play as a team and use the strength of all in their team over their need to be the best on the pitch. The children worked hard outside of lessons on their jobs and it really mattered to them. It cemented their learning because it had a real purpose.

I'm now trying to find ways to use this approach in English!

Year 6 class teacher

Finally, the Student-Designed Games model (Hastie 2010) for teaching physical education 'borrows' elements from each of the other models. Small 'learning teams' create their own games based upon some basic underlining principles such as: the games must aid skill development; they must be safe; they must include all and not eliminate players; participation and activity rates must be high; and all performers must be challenged, but have the chance to succeed. The benefits include greater game appreciation, increased fun and enjoyment, greater ownership over the game formats and increased social interaction. You act merely to facilitate the process from the periphery. 'The challenge is to be a facilitator, not a director, and to avoid being critical' (Hastie 2010, p. 27).

Children who already perceive physical education as being 'irresistible' are invariably those who have already developed a passion for sport, are often the more able performers and who are probably physically active both in and outside of school. Adopting different approaches to the teaching of physical education, using instructional models that are not always focused on developing physical skills in the practical domain, often provides opportunities for other 'less sporty' children to shine and view physical activity from a different perspective.

- Cross-curricular learning

CASE STUDY: Cross-curricular learning, example of adapting physical education lessons to embrace topic of Romans at White Cliffs Primary College for the Arts, Dover

The Year 4 children (8 – 9 years) had been studying the Romans as their 'topic' for the past term. In particular, they had enjoyed learning about the eruption of Mount Vesuvius and its destruction of Pompeii. In physical education the class had been exploring different balances and movement skills, seeking to combine them in short gymnastics sequences. Using the story of Pompeii as the theme for the lesson, half the class was asked to develop balances that represented the buildings and statues in the city while the rest were the lava, exploring different ways of (travel) moving in and around the city. The teacher even used a piece of music titled *Pompeii* by Bastille to enhance the experience.

Quick pause moment - Can you think of how you could integrate a physical education lesson into teaching one of the cross-curricular topics in your class?

CASE STUDY Cross-curricular learning, example of adapting physical education lessons to embrace topic of *The Folk of the Faraway Tree* at White Cliffs Primary College for the Arts, Dover

Year 2 (age 6–7 years) had thoroughly enjoyed reading Enid Blyton's *The Folk of the Faraway Tree* in literacy lessons and had used the characters in the book to develop extension writing and arts projects. The class teacher sought to harness this enthusiasm by developing the theme in her physical education lesson. Consequently, in creating different activity stations based around the characters who lived in the magic faraway tree she transformed a very simple throwing for accuracy lesson into an exciting and engaging set of 'Faraway Challenges'. One minute the children were 'helping Dame Washalot throw her dirty washing water down the tree' and the next they were 'throwing cherries into Mr Watizname's mouth'! The below are the activity stations used and the score sheet used within the lesson.

The Faraway Challenge – Score sheet

Character and part of the Magic Faraway Tree	Activity station	Attempt 1 score	Attempt 2 Score	Improvement Score
Throwing cherries into Mr Watizname's mouth	Target practice, throwing balls covered in Velcro onto target			
Knocking at the Angry Pixie's door	Target practice, throwing cricket ball to cricket stumps (5 points for hitting stumps)			
Knocking the fruit off the trees.	Hitting balls off cones with bean bags (2 points for every ball knocked off)			
Dame Washalot's washing basket	Throwing tennis balls into basket (2 points for every ball that lands in basket)			
Climbing the ladder to the top of the tree	Throwing bean bags into concentric hoops (3 points for each bean bag into hoop, 1 point for edge of hoop)			

Effective physical education lessons should not (ideally) be taught in isolation. For the subject to be truly valued and appreciated for the broad range of educational opportunities it delivers, you could look to see where physical education can be used to enhance learning in other areas of the curriculum through a cross-curricular approach. For example, there are so many links that can be made between science and physical education: Does science have to be taught in the classroom? Could you use your physical education environment to help support scientific knowledge and understanding to teach science in physical education or the other way round physical education in science? With many schools now adopting a 'topics' approach to teaching across different subject areas, why not include physical education? If the class is enthralled in learning projects developed around the studying the Victorian era, for example, why not teach a physical education lesson in the manner and format that Victorian children would have been taught? This approach to physical education can make lessons more exciting and engaging and may allow you to develop new approaches to teaching the subject.

How can you positively engage and encourage all children within physical education?

The SEND and Disability Act (2001) states that schools must take reasonable steps to ensure that disabled children are not placed at a substantial disadvantage in relation to the education and other services they provide. Plan strategically to increase the extent to which disabled children can participate in the curriculum. This may feel a little overwhelming when considering planning of physical education, but all you need to do is to think of our SRO model (Figure 3.1) – you as the 'sender' are just thinking and considering for all of your 'receivers'. So when you're planning, you are thinking how you would plan for the developmental stage that the children are at, their learning styles, their individual needs. It really isn't as scary as it may seem; it's just that we're not in a classroom anymore; all those 'good practice' elements and positive tactics that we would use in the classroom, we're now just going to use outside of the classroom; the way we differentiate into groups, we're just going to do that in physical education too. The key is to consider activities as more of how can the children access them, what support/additional resources are needed, or how can I adapt to include all. An example of the way to plan for supporting children with special educational needs is to consider the broad area of need, the types of learners, their characteristics and then inclusion strategies in physical education as per Table 3.2.

Traditionally high-jump competitions could be considered as being actually 'exclusive'. A jumper competes until they reach a height that they can no longer clear at which point they are declared 'out' of the competition. The better you are at your game, the more jumps you get; only the very best gets the most benefit from the activity, while those who need to practise more invariably get the least. A far more 'inclusive' approach can be seen in the case study discussed below in which a slanting rope is used. This creates different levels of challenge for the performer. Children can then choose which 'height' they jump, allowing everyone to achieve success with children progressing when they feel comfortable doing so. Pickup and Price (2007) suggest that every child brings a unique set of factors to physical education lessons and therefore carefully differentiated and inclusive tasks are needed within lessons.

Table 3.2 Thinking that could occur prior to planning, focusing on the needs of the children within your individual class

Supporting children with special educational needs:			
Broad areas of need (DfE, 2015)	**Types of learner:**	**Characteristics:**	**Inclusion strategies in physical education:**
Communication and Interaction (SLCN)			
Cognition and Learning			
Sensory and/or Physical needs			
Behavioural, Emotional and Social development			

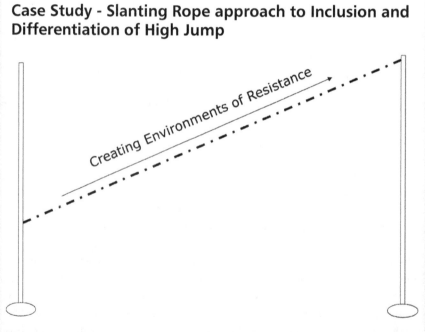

Case Study - Slanting Rope approach to Inclusion and Differentiation of High Jump

Creating Environments of Resistance

<u>Quick pause moment</u> – *Thinking about differentiation and using the idea of the case study above:*

Can you adopt the same differentiation approach to other movements, areas or skills of physical education?

How can you recreate the 'slanting rope' by differentiating the level of challenge for children with different abilities?

Table 3.3 STTEPs model for differentiation, adapted from Williams and Cliffe (2011, pp. 49–52).

SPACE	Adapting the working area to make it easier to perform a task	• In games, increase the space to allow children more reaction time and reduce space to encourage greater mobility and quicker thinking • Stand closer or further away from a partner when working together • Vary working pathways (straight/diagonal/zig zag) • Increase or decrease target areas to aim for
TASK	Each task is altered or is completely different to make it easier or more challenging	• Balance on large body parts • Or balance on small body parts • Dribble a hockey ball around cones • Or dribble up and down a straight line • Introduce different rules or roles for children (allow defenders to move from unopposed to opposed practice) • Stand still, run, walk, jog
TIME	Performing a skill more quickly or slowly. (Does not always need to be 'timed' using a stop watch)	• Limit the amount of touches of a ball before it must be passed • (Faster is not always more difficult) • For example, Gymnastics or dance routine done slowly with emphasis on the quality of moves
EQUIPMENT	Changing the resources can alter the difficulty of a task	• Use a slower moving object like a balloon to catch rather than a ball • Change the size/weight of the racket to make hitting easier • Use bean bags instead of balls • Use floats and armbands to aid swimming technique
PEOPLE	Generally the more the number of children involved in an activity the more difficult the activity becomes	• Play individually, in pairs, teams or groups • Keeping possession in a 3 v 2 practice is more challenging than 3 v 1 • More people in a dance makes it more difficult to choreograph
SAFETY	If you make changes to any of the STTEP components you may need to reinforce additional safety point; for example, 'You now have more people in a smaller space, remember to move with you head up looking for a space to get into.'	

    Differentiation strategies may seem daunting within physical education, but if you consider the STTEPs model it is possible to differentiate in multiple ways according to your children's needs. These can be through differentiating the use of space, the task itself, the time allowed for the activity, the equipment being used and the number of people involved in the activity. Table 3.3 shows an example of how the STTEPs model can be applied.

Summary

To conclude the chapter and to simplify what can be a very complex subject area for which there are a multitude of views and opinions and an inordinate array of research available, we have summarized the key points into 7 'P's for Perfect Pedagogy' adapted from the work of Launder (2001) for the purpose of making physical education 'irresistible':

- Preparation
- Pace
- Participation
- Progression
- Practice and Performance
- Personalized
- Positivity

Preparation

The best lessons are those that are well planned, with clear and visible objectives available for all to see. The lessons should form part of a progressive block or unit of work outlined in a medium and long-term planning document so that both you and the children are aware of the purpose of the lesson and where it 'fits' within their educational journey in physical education. You could carry small portable white boards with you to display the lesson objectives, regardless of where the lesson takes place. In order to help differentiation strategies and to provide motivational targets for children to achieve, learning objectives can be written in the 'AMS' format:

> **By the end of the lesson:**
>
> - ALL children will........
> - MOST children will.......
> - SOME children will...

Good teachers will refer to the objectives throughout the lesson to ensure that children know where they are making progress. Indeed, seeking some simple self-reflection from the children in the plenary at the end of the lesson with regard to who 'feels' they have achieved the different objectives can provide some very useful formative assessment in order to shape the learning for the following lesson. From a practical perspective, good preparation will ensure that there is adequate and appropriate equipment available at the beginning of the lesson. Where possible the working area is organized, cones can be laid out to organize the area and to make the area look exciting and engaging to the children as they arrive. You could think about how to best maximize the space available: Can you use existing court lines and walls to help facilitate the activities? How can transition between activities encourage progress within the lesson? Finally consideration needs to be made of the health and safety implications of working in different environments, whereby equipment and facilities are checked prior to use (see also Chapter 6).

Examples for 'irresistible' preparation and organization in lessons:

- Display objectives for all to see and make reference to them throughout the lesson
- Colour coordinate cones. This makes different working areas more visible to all
- 'Double up' when laying cones out. This will assist creating additional working areas of extending lines when needed
- Walk backwards laying cones to ensure lines are straight
- Make full use of court/playground lines (This also saves on use of cones)
- Engage fully with support staff before the lesson. This will enable them to be more proactive in dealing with situations as they arise, and feel more empowered in their role/responsibilities
- Prepare extension tasks for gifted and talented children and less challenging activities for the less able

Pace

Physical education is, by its very nature, an active subject. The Association for Physical Education (AfPE 2008) promotes the idea that physical education lessons should focus on children 'learning to move' and 'moving to learn'. Howells (2015) suggested that pace is key to keeping children 'engaged, positive and inspired' (p. 263). When delivering lessons, try to keep the children actively 'on task' for as long as possible, with less time spent on talking to the class or giving long, complex instructions. The transitions between tasks should be as efficient as possible. This requires forward thinking and planning to ensure that there is maximum utilization of all the available space and equipment, and so less children are waiting their 'turn'. Activities must be fun and engaging, but also relevant, so that children can appreciate the context of the task in their learning process. You could develop strategies to get the children's attention quickly and create effective organizational systems for changing, travelling to and from the location and for distributing and collecting equipment.

Examples for 'irresistible' Pace in lessons:

- Carry out organizational tasks while the children are getting changed.
- Create simple individual challenges/tasks for children to attempt while transitioning between activities and moving equipment. 'Try and balance the ball on the back of your hand? How long can you maintain the balance? Can you try your weaker hand?'

- Keep instructions to a minimum – use handouts to provide additional information or engage more able children to peer teach.

- Use the warm-up/cool-down activities as a means to distribute/collect equipment. 'See how many times you can keep bouncing the ball on your racket. When it drops, bring your racket and ball to the cupboard and put it away.'

- Use a simple tally chart system to calculate how many minutes of a lesson the children are 'active'.

- Ask the children questions about the lesson while they are getting changed at the end.

Participation

The need to foster high levels of physical activity within lessons in order to help improve children's health and fitness levels was discussed in the previous chapter. All children need to be actively involved in lessons for as much time as possible, including those who may be excused from the practical components of the lesson due to injury, for example. In order for learners to develop new skills they require lots of opportunities for meaningful practice and repetition. Launder (2001) uses two simple concepts to gauge the levels of participation in lessons. First, academic learning time-physical education (ALT-PE) is a crude measure of the effectiveness of teachers by comparing time spent talking or teaching with that spent actively practising, and research certainly suggests that most learning takes places when the children are actively 'doing' rather than listening. The second measure Launder introduces is maximum individual participation (MIP). This is a more effective way of assessing participation levels as it requires the observer to analyse specific individuals. For example, a group performing dribbling skills as part of a team relay would score highly on ALT-PE even though each individual has significant periods of inactivity while they wait for their turn (thus scoring lower on MIP). Regardless, you should seek to maximize both ALT-PE and MIP as a measure of good practice.

Examples for 'irresistible' Participation in lessons:

- Activator practical activities. All lessons should start with a fun and engaging 'activator' to raise heart rates and to prepare the class for the main part of the lesson. Simple tag or 'stuck in the mud' type games work well for this, but ideally they should be linked in some way to the main theme of the lesson. These activities also give you the opportunity to introduce the practical working area for the lesson (potentially outlining any safety considerations) and to introduce the theme and lesson objectives, links to previous learning and levels of expectation between bursts of activity.

- Maximize equipment. Where possible ensure every child has some equipment (for example, a ball) in order to maximize practice opportunities. Even if that means some children have slightly different equipment, it is better than simply waiting a turn.

- Line drills. Activities that require children to wait for their turn or 'line drills' reduce participation levels. As a rule, try to create activities whereby no more than four children are in a line at any time.

- Differentiation. This is one of most important considerations. Planning differentiated activities is the ability to maintain the interest and engagement of all children. Teachers will often prepare adapted activities to support the less able, but do not always seek to stretch the more able children (see also Chapter 8).

- Non-active participants. When planning lessons be sure to include those individuals who are unable to take a physically active role in lessons. Roles for non-participants could include them being officials or scorers for games activities. Could they be a 'coach' (see Sport Education Model) using reciprocal teaching resources to observe performance and provide guidance on specific areas for improvement? Additionally, should you seek to use technology to support the lesson, a role could be created that enables the 'non-doer' to film performances for analysis and feedback purposes, allowing them to learn cognitively and socially. Ultimately, learning in the practical domain (the 'doing' aspect of the physical education lesson) is only one area where learning takes place in a physical education lessons.

Progression

One of the first questions often reflected upon during lesson observations is 'Are the children making progress?' Williams (1996) defined three different ways in which progress within physical education lessons or units of works could be achieved: progression through 'difficulty', 'quality' or 'context' (Table 3.4):

To encourage progress, you should aim to gradually increase the level of challenge and complexity of tasks. When introducing new challenges or skills it is important that children achieve some level of success relatively quickly in order to give them the confidence to attempt more complex moves. As a simple rule for skill development you should try to progress from simple to complex. Therefore initial practices should be relatively simple and 'unopposed' in isolated (or 'closed') environments whereby the children can concentrate on the physical demands of the new skill before external challenges (such as the introduction of opposing players) make the activity more complex. Once a skill has been learnt in isolation, passive opponents may be gently introduced to create more game-like situations. By 'passive' it may mean they can be present but cannot 'tackle' or perhaps they can only walk. In order to develop confidence when dribbling to attack opponents, you may even try to use defenders as 'crabs' whereby they must sit on the floor and can only move sideways!

UNOPPOSED → PASSIVE → OPPOSED

Table 3.4 Three areas of progression within physical education, adapted from Williams (1996)

Progression through **Difficulty**	Children are required to perform increasingly challenging tasks	• Moving from single to combined movements (e.g. balance – balance to roll) • Moving from simple to advanced skills (e.g. basic throwing action – specialist throwing action – javelin) • Reduce the time and space available • Asking for a variety of ways of solving a problem (games tactic to beat defender in 2 v 1 situation)
Progression through **Quality**	Children demonstrate increasingly more sophisticated or successful performances	• Improved accuracy in target games • Increased fluency in skill performance • Better poise, control and form in gym or dance performances • Faster times or greater distance covered in athletic events
Progression through **Context**	Children carry out skills in increasingly complex situations	• Working individually, partners then groups • Understanding different roles within games • Taking greater responsibility for planning, performing and evaluating activities

Using observation (see Chapter 7) you can make formative judgements with regard to when they should 'move on'. However, the obvious signs are children becoming restless and losing focus in the task on hand. This is where effective differentiation strategies need to be employed; some individuals/groups will naturally progress quicker than others and to ensure that each one progresses at a level suited to their ability, teachers must be able to adapt activities quickly using the STTEPs model introduced previously.

Examples for 'irresistible' Progression in lessons:

● Use the introduction at the beginning of the lesson to set clear objectives and the plenary to evaluate 'progress' made by the class

● Use peer-coaching methods to enable individuals to receive personalized feedback from peers on how they can improve. (You may wish to consider creating simple checklists to help focus the coach on the correct aspects of performance that need coaching.)

● Seek to develop progression through overload – unopposed/passive/opposed

Practice and performance

Launder (2001) questioned the value of teachers who constantly resort to 'mindless games and dead-end drills' when teaching games (p. 21). His point is that practice, wherever possible, needs to mirror movements and activities from the real game or performance and the concept of 'transfer of training' suggests that the closer a practice situation aligns with reality, the more likely it is that new learning will transfer from practice to performance. What he means is within a lesson for warm-ups, progressions within the learning and cool down to all link together so learning can occur throughout all sections of the lesson. Good lesson organization and planning should provide children the chance to put their skills into a performance situation. Chapter 2 also outlined where and when competition can be used as an effective tool to enhance performance in physical education.

Examples for 'irresistible' Practice and Performance in lessons:

- It is the quality of practice rather than time involved that counts. Try to personalize both what is required from different individuals/teams through the use of differentiation strategies and the feedback each person receives on their performance.

- Teach children proper rules and format; to encourage them to accurately measure and assess each other's performances.

- When performing dance or gymnastics routines, look for the opportunity to have more than one group 'performing' at the same time in order to remove some of the apprehension some children may have if presenting to the whole class and to ensure you have asked the observers to look for specific dance and gymnastics skills and movements to comment on to help develop physical literacy and movement vocabulary.

- Also, ask groups to repeat their dance/sequence several times while 'performing', particularly if it is quite short in duration.

- Skills should be practised in the manner in which they are to be used in real situations. When practising, encourage lots of different variations of scenarios, team sizes and formations.

Positivity

Italian physician and educator Montessori once wrote: 'One test of the correctness of an educational procedure is the happiness of the child' (in Wright 2010, p. 45). Ultimately, the best way for you to make physical education 'irresistible' for children is to make it a fun and engaging experience.

Examples for 'irresistible' Positivity in lessons:

- Non-directive approach to teaching. Younger children, in particular, learn and develop through purposeful play (Almond and Lambden 2016, see also Chapter 1). If you can adopt a more creative and imaginary approach to teach skills that is meaningful to the children, we are far more likely to see greater engagement from them. As such, creating opportunities where the children can link cross-curricularly to other subjects or when children can use their imagination to be super heroes or Disney characters, thus making learning more fun, is more likely to keep them interested and focused.

- Mixed approach towards giving praise and recognition. Individual, isolated, in front of peers. You will know which children enjoy being put on a pedestal in front of their peers and are often motivated by the prospect of looking good in the eyes of others. Other children respond better to someone who takes the time to pull them one side and quietly recognize their efforts.

- Encourage greater responsibility. Children love to be a team captain (whatever that may entail) and the opportunity to wear the symbolic armband that goes with it. Why not create different armbands to allocate other responsibilities within a lesson. 'Mr Motivator' could be responsible for the class warm-up; 'Equipment Manager' could help organize equipment; 'Cheerleader' could be responsible for recognizing and praising others.

- Challenges and personal bests. There is a saying that suggests that 'if a child can score a goal every day, they will always come back some more to play'. Individual goals and targets, particularly if self-created, can enable all children to succeed at their own level, regardless of how they compare to others.

- Positive Praise Rewards. Many schools have amazing programmes designed to acknowledge and reward good effort and performance in schools. One school has invested in a programme entailing 'positive praise postcards' and teachers are encouraged to mail one postcard each week to the parents of deserving children of every group they teach. Likewise, within lessons, inspiration was taken from referees who brandish yellow and red cards to create a series of positive cards to recognize 'best behaviours': effort, teamwork, continued improvement and sportsmanship. This has an even greater impact when teachers ask children to give the cards out to their peers (Figure 3.4).

- Positive Praise Circle. At the end of a lesson ask the class to organize themselves into groups of seven or eight children and for the groups to stand in a circle facing each other. Give one person in each circle a ball, ask them to say something positive about somebody else in the circle and pass that person the ball. That person must repeat the process, praising someone else

Figure 3.4 Positive Praise Cards

Figure 3.5 Physical education board

in the circle. This encourages the group to understand and recognize the contributions each individual can make within a lesson.

- Students of the month. Create noticeboards where a 'student of the month' could be displayed, along with a short piece of text outlining why the reward was given. These strategies can be linked to other whole-school reward programmes. See Figure 3.5 for the physical education board within a primary school that displayed successes in the school games.

The next chapter will examine how to promote success within physical education as a practical activity. It will examine how to structure lessons, as well as offer suggestions on ways to plan to ensure all children learn successfully.

Recommended reading

The following three texts are provided as follow-on reading:

1 OFSTED (2013). Beyond 2012 – outstanding physical education for all. Physical education in schools 2008–12. (Available at www.ofsted.gov.uk/resources/120367).

2 Launder, A. (2001). Play Practice: The Games Approach to Teaching and Coaching Sports. Champaign, IL; Leeds: Human Kinetics. (Chapter 7)

3 Metzler, M. W. (2011). Instructional Models for Physical Education (3rd edn). Scottsdale, AZ: Holcomb Hathaway.74959601161000

Sample lesson plans for a sport education scheme of work

River Primary School

Year Group Themed Unit Planner – Medium and Short-Term Plan – Lesson Sequence

NAME OF THEME: Sport Education   Unit start date: 6.11.15 Unit end date: 11.12.15

Planning and Preparation

The underlying key to good teaching is good planning based on thorough assessment and sound subject knowledge.

Full familiarity with the plan and lesson content promotes professional confidence to make adaptations during the lesson to meet presenting needs while still achieving good pace and new learning.

Long-term planning – The National Curriculum and the school's curriculum map are the reference documents.

Medium-term planning – Teachers consider whether units are discrete, linked or continuous and plan learning on the following format appropriately.

Short-term planning – Modifications to planned lessons are made according to assessments and evaluations shown as annotations.

Self-reflection for planning:

- Is my lesson going to engage, inspire and excite children, moving learning forward?
- Is my subject knowledge sufficient to ensure that at least good learning takes place for each child?
- Have I planned appropriate differentiated activities?
- Do success criteria focus on the right knowledge, skills and understanding?
- How does the lesson contribute to the development of basic skills – reading, writing, communication, maths?
- How will children be encouraged to plan for successful learning? How will they work? What skills will they need?
- During the lesson – how will I directly teach a focus group but support and encourage all learners equally?
- During the lesson do I assess learners against the learning objective and note this on the plans?
- Does my plenary engage all learners, reflect sufficiently on new learning and enable me to assess understanding?
- Have I used my formative assessment to record significant achievements?

Self-reflection for teaching and learning

Teaching: Do I keep the pace snappy? Max 10 minutes only.

Have I made clear to them the expectations of pace, standards and outcome?

Learning: Have I planned activities for the whole class, small groups or targeted individuals?

Have I identified one focus group where I will accelerate learning?

Do I also move around the class at intervals to provide feedback, talk and teach and keep pupils on task?

Do I use time targets throughout? For example, 'five more minutes to finish this section'.

Am I ensuring that I remain focused on all learners throughout the lesson?

Plenary: Have I used this part of the lesson to review and assess what I have taught and what has been learnt by the pupils?

Do pupils internalize their learning by verbalizing their views, ideas and understanding when they report to the rest of the class? Do I use 'think pair share'?

Do pupils share successes and problems?

Do all learners sometimes take the lead in reporting to the class, to increase their confidence and independence as learners?

Subject Games 6.11.15

Term 2 wk 1 Focus children:

Main Objective – linked to programme of study

Coach Objectives	Teaching content/strategies	Plenary
LO: To develop dribbling skills with a football and practise a range of techniques for changing direction	Lesson introduction Discuss with class that this term's football will follow a sport education model. Children will be divided into four teams and will remain in this team for duration of term. Each child adopts a role: coach, fitness coach x2, referee, results analyst, player, equipment. Children are working towards developing and improving skills required within football and towards a final tournament. Who will be best suited for each role? What have you got to offer your team? What is your strong point? Allocate roles. Coaches to be given LO and discuss with CT skills and drills needed to achieve objective	AFL Questions: See main body of plan
	In Classroom: Reminder for expectations about 'being safe' and undertake health and safety check by CT and children.	
Success Criteria Children (Chn) to adopt roles Chn to develop dribbling skills including change of direction	Warm-up: Fitness coaches to lead warm-up. Ensuring aerobic game/activity to raise heart rate – why do we need to raise heart rate? What happens to our bodies during this process? Rotation of joints – why do we raise heart rate first? CT and TA to observe groups ensuring correct outcome. Opportunities for pupils to become physically confident in a way which supports their health and fitness	
	Play: Coaches (AA) to give teams time to explore dribbling and passing skills. What do you notice from your team? How are you going to develop them? Which part of your foot should you be using? Master basic movements and begin to apply these in a range of activities	
Vocabulary Sport Education Roles Teamwork	Teach: Coaches to demonstrate correct dribbling and passing skills to own team. What do you notice about their bodies? Which part of their foot do they use? Are they able to pass accurately? Why? Continue to apply and develop a broader range of skills, learning how to use them in different ways and to link them to make actions and sequences of movement	
	Play: Children to select appropriate skills to dribble and pass the ball accurately. Were you more successful? Why? How have you improved? Develop an understanding of how to improve in different physical activities and sports	
	Cool down – fitness coaches to lead cool down ensuring all child perform cool-down activity and stretches.	
	Review: How did you work as a team? How will you improve this next week? Enjoy communicating, collaborating and competing with each other	
	Sportsmanship, teamwork, LO achieved and perseverance points awarded. Upto 10 points can be awarded for each section which are all counted towards the final score at the end of the tournament.	
	CT and TA to observe and provide support at all times offering feedback on ways to improve and develop teamwork and achieve LO	
Resources Footballs And any other equipment required by teams	Group 1 To develop leadership skills. To support and develop other team members. To develop independent learning.	Group 2 To develop independent learning, to understand working and supporting within a team.	Group 3 To develop independent learning, to understand working and supporting within a team
	Assessment	Assessment	Assessment
Lesson Evaluation		

Main Objective – linked to programme of study.

Subject Games 13.11.15

Term 2 wk 2

Focus children Lo given to coaches on Fri 6.11.15

Coach Objectives	Teaching content/strategies	Plenary
To become more accurate with passing and receiving skills	(including differentiated activities for AA/A/Focus/BA/SEN)	Plenary
To perform skills more fluently and effectively in games.	Lesson introduction What drill will you use? How will this support the LO? Make sure you perform the skill of passing and receiving and NOT shooting. How will you do this? Play a small-sided game? Don't forget to use your referee ensuring development of their skills. Come and discuss your drills and ideas with me beforehand to ensure LO will be achieved.	AFL Questions: See main body of plan
Success Criteria	LO discussed between coaches and CT. Coach plans attached	
Chn able to pass more accurately	In Classroom: Reminder for expectations about 'being safe' and undertake health and safety check by CT and children.	
Chn able to pass and receive more effectively	Warm-up: fitness coaches to lead aerobic game to raise heart rate. Why do we need to raise heart rate? What effects does exercise have on our bodies? Plan attached Perform rotation of joints. Opportunities for pupils to become physically confident in a way which supports their health and fitness	
Vocabulary	Play: Children to explore through skills and drills – each coach to deliver planned sessions ensuring teaching point on plans are demonstrated and understood by all members of team. CT and TA to observe and support when required.	
Pass	Develop a broader range of skills, learning how to use them in different ways	
Receive	Teach: Coach to demonstrate correct action to pass and receive the ball correctly. What do you notice? How will you implement this skill? Develop competence to excel in a broad range of physical activities	
Accurate	Play: Children to select appropriate skills required to pass and receive ball more accurately. Can your team pass and receive while walking/running?	
	Teams to play small-sided modified games to consolidate accurate passing and receiving skills rehearsed during drills. Engage in competitive sports and activities 3 successful passes = 1 point.	
	Cool down – fitness coaches to lead cool down ensuring all children perform cool-down activity and stretches.	
	Review: Did you achieve your LO? How did you work as a team? What went well/needs improving? Compare their performances with previous ones and demonstrate improvement	
	Sportsmanship, teamwork, LO achieved and perseverance points awarded. Up to 10 points can be awarded for each section; all points count towards the final score at the end of the tournament.	
	CT and TA to observe and support at all times offering feedback on ways to improve and develop teamwork and achievement of LO	
Resources	Group 1 To develop leadership skills. To support and develop other team members. To develop independent learning.	Group 2 To develop independent learning, to understand working and supporting within a team. To improve accurate passing and receiving in football.
Footballs		Group 3 To develop independent learning, to understand working and supporting within a team, to improve passing and receiving in football.
And any other equipment required by teams		
	Assessment	Assessment
		Assessment

Chapter 4
Physical Education as a Practical Activity

Chapter objectives

- Physical education as a practical activity
- Learning through inquiring
- How to develop these inquiry skills within lessons?
- How physical education can allow children to problem solve and inquire through their physical settings?

Introduction

This chapter will consider physical education as a practical activity and examine how to ensure that children learn successfully in primary physical education lessons. This chapter analyses the teacher's role in making success happen, in particular how to promote success. The chapter will also explore the concept of inquiry teaching and provide examples of how this may be introduced within lessons. This chapter intends to provoke thought and reflection and encourages you (as a teacher/practitioner) to reflect upon your own practice and implement some of the concepts and strategies that are presented. The focus is to develop understanding of how all children can benefit from inquiry-based teaching and learning and to provide a framework for the teacher to develop additional delivery skills to complement their existing practice.

Physical education as a practical activity

One would assume that this topic of physical education as a practical activity needs no explanation! Surely physical education must be practically based and those participating be full of active children? The answer is, of course, yes, in lessons where there is high-quality learning and teaching. However, a further look into the word 'active' in physical education in schools is required. Being vigorously active, that is, getting out of breath should occur for 50 per cent of the time allocated for a physical education lesson (Fairclough et al. 2008), as previously discussed in further detail in Chapter 2. There are also many other objectives of physical education apart from activity levels. Learning of skills, for example, is a necessary component of physical education but may be in direct conflict with the concept of high activity (Carroll and Loumidis 2001). You must therefore consider and 'way up' the balance between maximizing the amount of activity that occurs within the lesson and the amount of learning and understanding that takes place. This is supported by MacAllister (2013), who suggests that 'physical education should be defined in such a way that it depends on pupil physical activity for the sake of valuable learning and development'. (p. 909)

Active also implies a degree of engaged involvement, so there will be a number of occasions when children may not be physically performing but are still actively engaged in learning. These occasions may be only short periods, but are important as they allow children to observe, evaluate, umpire, coach or score, but we must ensure that they are actively engaged. This is still being active and learning within the lesson and in a practical context. The important point here is that the experience is 'rounded'; the child is being educated wholly through a practical experience which is mostly active and not sedentary.

Promoting success

One of the key considerations that is fundamental to high-quality teaching and learning in physical education is the principle of making children successful. When planning lessons do you explicitly think about what being successful looks like in that lesson, within the skills, activity or movement? If the answer is yes, then you are truly trying to be inclusive and provide an engaging, differentiated experience for children to learn, have fun and progress. Bravo! However, if the answer is no, not sure or maybe, then some further exploration of this topic is required to inform thinking. Let us consider this situation from a different perspective. Regardless of the subject it is highly likely that a class of children will display a range of abilities, knowledge and confidence. If, for instance, you were to examine how you may teach writing, there will be a range of strategies and resources available to build writing skills. Some children will make faster progress than others and there is the need to provide these children with the right amount of challenge, variety, engagement, feedback and praise that keeps them interested and confident to do more. This will then build success for the child. Some of the strategies that may be used may not actually involve writing; for example, children may read, draw a picture of their favourite book, tell their partner some interesting news or present something to the class. All of these activities draw upon a range of skills that promote and help to improve and make the child a successful writer. Successful and improved writing is the end product, but the journey (depending upon the child) may be quite varied.

The same concepts and ideas to promoting success apply in physical education. There are many skills required to be developed within physical education, and (as discussed in Chapter 6) it is recognized that not all of these skills require high physical ability. Some skills will be learnt through thinking (cognitive), interacting (social) or understanding how feelings and emotions (affective) relate to oneself and others (Laker 2000). So, as with the writing example, it is important that you ensure that a range of practical experiences are pitched at the right level to engage the child, making the child feel that they will have some degree of success and will make progress. For example, it is unlikely that you would ask a class of thirty children to do exactly the same thing when they write a story. You would probably give them a topic, ask them to make up a character or consider a certain issue or perspective in their writing. As teachers you can provide structural guidance if required and then allow their creativity to take over. You may allow some pictures or the use of technology to aid success, that is, the task is differentiated. Yet, when the same class is in physical education do you provide choice and support and make all the equivalent things available to them as you previously did when they were writing in the classroom? Or do you ask them to do virtually the same thing such as pass a ball in the same way or all roll across the mat in the same direction or all run the same distance? These examples are generalized here to emphasize a point which is twofold.

First, all children are different (which is a given), but just like in any other subject, we must ensure that when they perform physical education lessons they feel that they can be successful regardless of their ability; we must teach them that although the subject is a physical one there are other components of it in which they can excel. We must educate them about what being successful in physical education in their school means. If nothing else, we should create a physical education environment where all children feel physically and emotionally safe and they understand that they have a contribution to make to their own and others safety or well-being (Figure 4.1). Recognizing and celebrating the skills of the leader, organizer, umpire, scorer, etc. are just as valuable as physical talent and performance. Physical education is multi-dimensional and there should be something for everyone. The learning through this range of skills (along with the physical) provides the child with a broader experience and understanding of themselves through the medium of physical education. This may then provide the child incentive to continue to participate in sports beyond school, into adult years. This supports the concept of the physically literate child (Whitehead 2010). We must encourage participation and success to promote lifelong physical activity.

The way in which lessons are structured is vital. Chapter 5 looks in more detail at lesson plans and structures. Regardless of your subject knowledge or confidence to teach physical education you must recognize and draw strength from your own knowledge of how you differentiate and manage the learning and classroom resources in the subjects where you feel **most confident** and have the **most success**. This should then be harnessed and taken with you when you step into the physical education environment. You are already aware of the principles of high-quality learning and

Figure 4.1 Children working together in a safe environment to complete the nightline course as one whole team

teaching and they do not significantly change across subjects and you could reflect on and recognize what you are good at and use this as a vehicle for delivering lessons in subjects where you are less confident. Physical education is a place where there is more noise, movement and potential for accidents and these areas can often be seen as factors that impact on confidence levels, but you need to remember that you have the classroom management and resource skills already but you may not be making the connection between your existing skills and how these skills may be utilized in physical education. Naturally there may be some additional knowledge and an understanding of any safety issues in the specific subject area may be required. In Table 4.1 there are examples of existing skills which are used in other subjects and how they can be transferred to physical education (Have a go at the Science section in the table, what do you do really well that you can transfer into physical education?).

With both experienced teachers and those training to be teachers, there is often a great deal of deliberation around lesson or learning objectives and how best to write them. It is often easy to pose the following question to yourself: 'What does the learning look like by the end of the lesson – what will the child/children be doing, showing or saying?' For some having the question helps them to then articulate the answer quite clearly, but many others are stumped by this question. If you are stumped by it, then think about the end of the lesson and what desired outcome is required and work backwards in the planning. In this way the last thing that is written will be the learning objectives. The lesson will have been clearly thought out with the right level of activity, challenge, progression, differentiation and support. There will be clear links and transitions between activities ensuring achievement and success for everyone. Picturing the end of the lesson is crucial for the initial

Table 4.1 – Teacher/classroom skills in different subjects transferable to physical education

Subject	Teacher/classroom skills	Transfers to physical education	Success for children
Literacy	Teacher creates opportunities for discussion and children make judgements on the quality of their work	Teacher creates opportunities for discussion and children make judgements on the quality of their work	Children can work independently and understand how to evaluate their own performance and that of others
Design and Technology	Children are aware of the dangers of using tools and can use them safely	Teacher explains the meaning of safety in physical education using a range of equipment	Children can use a range of equipment safely and can avoid dangerous situations
Art	Teacher manages multiple activities with a wide range of equipment	Teacher manages multiple activities with a wide range of equipment	Availability of a range of activities and/or equipment offers wider choice to children, promoting progress and success
Numeracy	Teacher groups children by ability	Existing numeracy groups work together in physical education during an activity, that is, problem-solving	Children learn team work towards a specific goal using a range of skills within the group
Science			

stages of lesson planning. Lawrence (2012) suggests that teachers should picture the end of the lesson and understand what children need to achieve. This allows them to think about how the picture will develop and the order in which activities or events may need to happen. In essence what is being suggested here is a type of reverse engineering. Figure 4.2 is a suggestion of how the reverse engineering of learning objectives might look. It is not a detailed plan but more of a framework which promotes thought but which also allows flexibility so that it can be applied across any medium or any activity or any age within physical education. The model is straightforward. Working through numbers 1–6, each box should be considered in turn to provide a step-by-step framework which leads to deciding the learning objectives of the lesson as the last part of the planning process. In this way the whole lesson should be structured so that all children gain success in achieving the learning objective.

The provision of processes, models and frameworks is all well and good but there is often a disconnection between these and the reality of planning. Therefore, the template (Table 4.2) is a simplified lesson plan that could be used. I have also provided a simplified lesson plan to illustrate the reverse engineering model in action. A little

Figure 4.2 Reverse engineering model of learning objectives

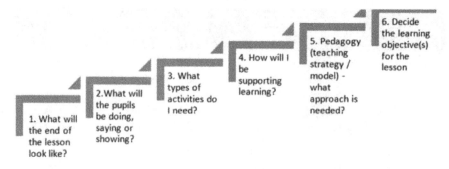

Table 4.2 Template of reverse engineering model within a lesson plan format

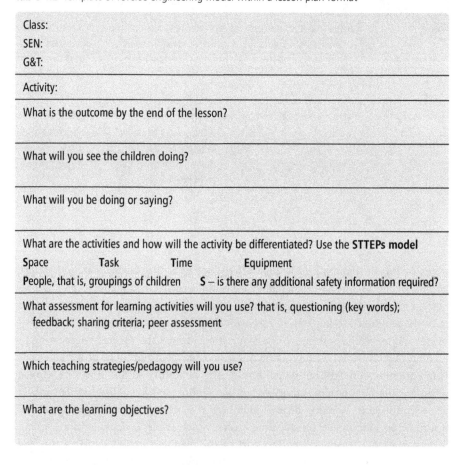

Class: SEN: G&T:
Activity:
What is the outcome by the end of the lesson?
What will you see the children doing?
What will you be doing or saying?
What are the activities and how will the activity be differentiated? Use the **STTEPs model** Space   Task   Time   Equipment People, that is, groupings of children   **S** – is there any additional safety information required?
What assessment for learning activities will you use? that is, questioning (key words); feedback; sharing criteria; peer assessment
Which teaching strategies/pedagogy will you use?
What are the learning objectives?

detail has been added to help to demonstrate that the reverse engineering model is a series of steps which can be dropped into existing lesson plans as headings. The example is not designed to be a 'gold' standard template but is aimed at showing how this process is not designed to be burdensome and can be implemented quite easily and used to support planning.

Pause for thought – *Thinking about successful opportunities*

How will you build skills and confidence to create successful opportunities, to get children to successfully meet the learning objective?

What would you plan for, to build in skills and confidence? Does it make you think about learning objectives in a different way?

Building upon the previous ideas of Lawrence (2012), another concept to be considered in the delivery of practical lessons is to try to identify what is the most important part of the lesson from a learning perspective, that is, what is the part of the lesson where the lesson or learning objectives start to be met by the children? This will arguably be dependent upon the learning objective, and this may be at any point of the lesson. Crucial to achieving the learning objective is matching an appropriate activity so that learning can happen and determining what the teacher will do to support the learning. In trying to imagine the end product of the lesson, it is vital to understand and identify a key moment or moments that lead to children being successful. This can be best explained as the 'moment' by labelling it as the **pivotal learning window (PLW)** which is explained in Figure 4.3.

The pivotal learning window can be used to identify the key moment(s) of learning within a lesson. These may be the main activity taking a significant amount of lesson time. The term 'pivotal' is used rather than optimal as optimal suggests that there is

Figure 4.3 Pivotal learning window

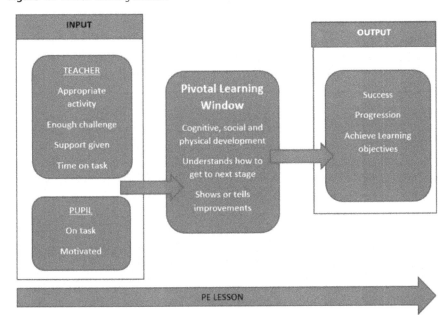

an exact moment within the lesson. This is not the case because the pivotal learning window may be experienced at different times within the lesson or a key activity by children of differing abilities. The term 'pivotal' is used as it is reliant upon input from the teacher and the child. Without this input (teacher, student or both) it is unlikely that the learning objectives will be achieved in full. The term 'window' is used to recognize that learning is not a fixed point and as such the 'window' of time in which significant learning takes place in relation to the learning objectives may be longer for some children than others or in fact learning may happen earlier in the lesson than expected. If this happens, our use of formative assessment and questioning should allow for additional tasks to be set.

Learning through inquiring

As mentioned earlier in the chapter, it is important as a practitioner to visualize the end of the lesson to recognize the key features/activities that make it a successful lesson and plan accordingly. It is also important to consider to what extent do children really understand what the activity looks like and what are they aiming to achieve from it? What are the significant learning moments in the lesson and are they guided and supported in the right way so that they are 'tuned in' to how you want them to learn. This will only occur if you start to share more of your thoughts, ideas and concerns about how they are learning. Most children will have seen the game of football, for example, and will have seen some kind of high-quality match so they can create a picture in their mind of the rudiments of the game but perhaps fewer children will have seen a good dance or gymnastics performance. Moreover, it is likely that there may even be teachers who have limited knowledge and or experiences of dance and outdoor and adventure education. So, when picturing the key moments of the lesson and then planning towards that moment(s), how much consideration is given to determining what children know about the activity? Pickup and Price (2007) support this concept stating, in determining objectives for pupils' learning, two further questions need to be addressed, namely 'What do the children already know?' and 'What will the children be able to learn in the future?'(p. 100).

Therefore, it is important to assume that children have some knowledge, at least of their own capabilities and/or of the activity within the lesson itself. This prior knowledge is likely to be acquired from either being an observer or a participant. For example, the teacher may introduce an activity to the children by saying, 'Everyone here has the potential to be a dancer. You will be successful if you can perform a dance pattern by linking actions together with control to tell a story.' Within primary physical education lessons, most dance actions can be improved by extension of the arms and legs and having good posture and control over movement patterns (see also Chapter 6 which looks at developing skills and in particular dance in further detail). This will help children to improve the realism of the movement patterns and the story that they are telling which in turn will be more obvious to their audience. In this way we are drawing upon previous movement knowledge which can then be used to develop quality and confidence in all children to recognize that they can dance. Figure 4.4 shows Mathew Prichard as a young child aged five being inspired and encouraged to dance; he attended dance classes both within school as an after-school class where he was the only boy, but was encouraged that he 'could' and he also attended dance classes in the community with his sister Rebeca. He is now is finishing his final year at Rambert School of Ballet and Contemporary Dance in London (Figure 4.5).

In this dance example the emphasis is that everyone can be successful (such as Mathew) in an activity where there can be preconceived ideas of what is required to make children think that they either 'can' or 'cannot'. Our role as teachers is to provide the necessary opportunity and support so that they can. You are inspiring the next generation of professional athletes. This is why it is imperative that the learning objective is suitable. It is important that children understand that they can dance and are supported to do so ensuring that we build confidence which is likely to encourage children to try other activities. This will build a culture that promotes learning as a

Figure 4.4 'Little' Mathew, 5yrs, with his elder sister Rebeca at home, practising their dance finish positions for his first-ever dance school community show

Figure 4.5 'Big' Mathew, in his last year at Rambert, an inspired and successful leading dancer

team effort between the child and the teacher and/or child to child. This is a powerful dynamic which will inspire and excite learners in physical education.

Another factor in developing understanding in physical education is for children to recognize the links between areas of activity within physical education and the transferrable skills that can be utilized. Children should also be able to recognize and distinguish between each activity area of physical education and understand how they are distinct and specific to that activity area. In addition to recognizing that there are links between each area of physical education, teachers should also be able to articulate the distinctiveness of each area of physical education and recognize the specific contribution that each makes to the child's physical education. Below are some of the unique qualities of each activity area that children should understand:

- **Games** – understanding and applying strategies of attack and defence
- **Gymnastics** – quality of actions; performing fluid sequences, body awareness
- **Dance** – conveying meaning; artistic expression
- **Athletics** – maximum output
- **Outdoor Education** – challenge and problem-solving in different environments;
- **Swimming** – all of the above qualities can be developed through water safety, polo, diving, synchronized swimming, racing and personal survival.

Inquiry-based teaching

Inquiry-based teaching stems predominantly out of science education and aims to develop challenging situations in which children are asked to observe and question constructs, posture explanations of what they observe; devise and conduct experiments in which data are collected to support or refute their theories; analyse data; draw conclusions from experimental data; design and build models; or any combination of these types of activities. As such, these types of learning experiences are designed to be open-ended in that children are not expected to simply reach the 'right' or 'correct' answer for the question they are confronted with. When an inquiry-based teaching method is being used, the teacher is more concerned with student 'processes' of reaching their conclusion. Ward and Roden (2008) recommended especially for young children of infant age (5–7 years) that inquiring is completed on a daily basis as it equips infants with the capabilities to discover information throughout life.

In a physical education context, inquiry-based teaching approaches are often used when children already have a basic understanding of sports and games. You could use this teaching strategy to help children understand when to apply certain skills. What to do when they are not in possession of the ball, or where they can best move to receive a ball, or defend against a pass to name a few examples. Inquiry-based teaching can be used to foster children's critical thinking in game situations and provide them with the opportunities to explore games and sports in new and innovative ways. However, if children do not have the basic understanding, proficiency and application of motor skills, the inquiry-based teaching approach may not be an appropriate teaching strategy.

How to develop these inquiry skills within lessons

Providing children open-ended problems (or questions) gives them the opportunity to use enquiry to explore a problem. A degree of ambiguity may be needed here to allow the children to discuss the problem from a variety of perspectives and explore solutions that are not the norm. This provides real evaluative moments where the children can then decide how successful they are in relation to the task and adjust accordingly. To do this a clear understanding of pedagogical models (as discussed in Chapter 3) and teaching styles used in physical education and how they complement each other is required.

Pause for thought – *Thinking about planning*

When planning physical education lessons how might you utilize different teaching styles, methods or pedagogies to help children to learn?

What might you have to change in your own practice to do this?

Pedagogy to support inquiry

Physical education is often led by the teacher (Kinchin in Bailey 2010) through the use of the teacher-directed model. This model is particularly useful when teaching new skills and there are specific safety instructions that need to be strictly adhered to such as in swimming, athletics or outdoor education. However, in this model the teacher has high input to the lesson. Alternative pedagogical models have been designed over the years such as Student Designed Games (Hastie 2010), Cooperative Learning (Dyson and Casey 2012), Teaching Games for Understanding (Thorpe and Bunker and Almond 1982) and Sport Education (which are discussed further in Chapter 3). These models place the child at the centre of the learning and teaching process whereby they have high input and the teacher plays more of a facilitation role. How these models link to support inquiry is explored in further detail below.

Student-designed games must:

- Contribute to skill development
- Include, not eliminate – those who are usually first eliminated have least skills and need most practice
- Have high participation rates
- Be structured so that all children can be successful and are challenged
- FUN – involves all participants at an appropriate level of challenge (skills and tactics)
- FAIR – Success (scoring) should not be too easy or too hard to achieve. There needs to be balance between defence and offense so neither dominates
- SAFE – Games have rules that keep participants safe and children are not embarrassed or humiliated

Adapted from Hastie (2010)

Cooperative Learning Model – Five components to support inquiry (Dyson and Grineski 2001)

Team Formation

Diversity of group: Learning in groups that are heterogeneous in gender, race, economic status and ability. Begin with pairs as this allows for maximum participation and communication, then transition into a larger group.

Positive Interdependence

Each group member depends on others to complete the task, for example, pairing up to complete a joint task. Recognition that different roles contribute different things to the group success.

Individual Accountability

Individual children should not get lost in the group activities. Each child is accountable for their learning. You can question children, ask for explanations, encourage peer teaching or complete written work.

Positive Social Interaction Skills

Listening to each other. Shared decision making. Taking responsibility for jobs. Giving and receiving feedback. How to positively encourage each other.

Group Processing

The 'debrief' – what happened? So What? What next? Time allocated to discuss whether group members are achieving their goals and working well together.

How can physical education allow children to problem solve and inquire through their physical settings?

The importance of questioning to evidence learning

A useful way to develop inquiry skills is to create a range of generic open-ended questions that may be used to engage children. However, it is necessary to have a range of questions that is specific to the age of the children and the activity so a vocabulary can be built up. Closed questions can also be used to build subject-specific knowledge. This is important because without consideration we may ask the following question: 'Say one thing that's good and one thing that needs to be improved.'

Initially this seems quite a reasonable question, but is it appropriate to use the same question with all year groups? Where is the progression in the level of questioning if it is always the same? It could be argued that the same question given to different year groups would elicit a different response. Instead, ensure that the questions asked are related to the learning and language of the lesson and the learning objective and allow children to be analytical in relation to this and see how successful they think they are being. This would allow the question to be easily adapted but specific and focused within the lesson context. For example: 'Say one thing that was good about the use of directions within the motif and one thing that needs to be improved on in terms of pathways.'

Kline (1999) proposed that 'a question works because, unlike a statement which requires you to obey, a question requires you to think. The mind seems to prefer to think, not obey.'

So the questions that are asked should try to:

- develop interest and motivate children to become actively involved in lessons;
- develop critical thinking skills and inquiring attitudes;
- stimulate children to pursue knowledge on their own.

Here are some examples of questions (in no particular order) to use with children in physical education:

- Which action is better and why?
- What might you do differently next time to make it better?
- What did you do to make your actions smooth and flowing?
- Can you watch your partner and do the same as them?
- Can you describe exactly what you can see?
- Can you tell me the difference between your performance and your partner's performance?
- Can you use keywords from today's lesson to say what you see your partner doing?
- What does it feel like when you do those movements?
- Why have you chosen those movements?

As you can see, these questions are generic. In this way there is a variety of questions to be used, and they can be used across a range of activities which will provide consistency to questioning within lessons. You can also supplement these questions with lesson- or activity-specific questions (Table 4.3).

Pause for thought – *Thinking about questioning:*

Can you design some generic questions of your own?

Perhaps work with the year group above and below your class to develop progression in questioning.

Can you observe a colleague and see how they use questioning within their lesson?

Table 4.3 Generic and specific question examples

Generic	Specific
'We are learning…..' - when referring to learning objectives.	'We are learning which balances are easier to link and which are more difficult.'
'Remember to …' – when referring to success criteria	'Remember to use tension/extension and hold your balance for 5 seconds.'
'I can …' when assessing the learning outcomes.	'I can perform a handstand and then link it to a forward roll'

Use of limited instructions to develop inquiry skills

Another way is to give children limited instructions when setting a problem. The reason behind this is that you will provide enough information so that they can understand the task and learn safely. This makes the learning more experiential and children will have to consider the information that they need to know before completing the task. Giving a lot of information may narrow the focus too much and hinder creative thought and/or the learning journey. If you are brave enough to try this it is also important that you can

- ask quality questions to promote thought
- step out of the lesson and observe what is happening
- not fill the silence
- allow child thinking/planning time (perhaps with limited input from you)

Historically problem-solving activities have sat in the realm of outdoor and adventurous activities and have been a component of the physical education curriculum in schools in the UK. Gruber (1986), and more recently Howells and Bowen (2016), found evidence that physical education had a positive influence on self-esteem. It is also important to remember that inquiry is not specific to problem-solving and should be encouraged across all activity areas within physical education. If problem-solving activities are common place then the ability of the children to transfer inquiry skills and use them in a wide range of situations can only be beneficial to the development of independent thinkers and learners which will justify further claims suggesting that physical education can 'contribute towards the integrated development of mind and body ... positively enhance self-confidence and self-esteem; enhance social and cognitive development and academic achievement' (Talbot (2001), in MacFayden and Bailey 2002, p. 3).

Skills to support and develop inquiry

The Tables 4.4 and 4.5 are examples of how to use simple skills grid to develop inquiry-based opportunities with Key Stage 2. The caveat here is that there will need to be a degree of direction and control in the organization due to the age of the children. The permutations offered by the grid, in conjunction with the types of questions asked, should support learners in developing their physical enquiry skills. The Tables 4.4 and 4.5 are split into two sections – *equipment and target. Equipment* can be used on its own to allow children to use a range of resources or both sections can be used. The amount of equipment and targets used can be reduced depending upon the year group. Children can be challenged by asking them questions which will create opportunities for them to undertake. Supplementary questions can be posed to develop high level thinking and deepen understanding.

Table 4.4 Games skills grid with focus on equipment

Skills	Equipment				
	Racket and ball	Smaller ball	Larger ball	Stick/bat and ball	Quoit
Rolling					
Throw under arm					
Throw over arm					
Throw up → catch					
Throw up → bounce					
Bowling					
Bouncing					
Hitting					
Kicking					

Table 4.5 Games skills grid with focus on target

Skills	Target						
	Rope	Hoop	Bucket/box	Skittle/cones	Wall/post	Person	Space
Rolling							
Throw under arm							
Throw over arm							
Throw up → catch							
Throw up → bounce							
Bowling							
Bouncing							
Hitting							
Kicking							

Supplementary questions for equipment include

- Choose a piece of equipment that you would like to use?
- Show me how you will use it.
- Can you find out how you can use it with different parts of your body?

- Get with a partner and find out what they can do.
- Design a way of using your equipment with your partner.
- How successful were you?
- What will make it even better?

Children can be encouraged to choose equipment and how they will engage with it. For example, using a quoit to throw up and catch or hitting a smaller ball with a stick or racket. It is experimental, but will allow the children to show you what they can do and keep them engaged through choice which can be progressed.

Supplementary questions for equipment and target include

- Choose a target that you would like to use.
- Choose three different pieces of equipment and work out which one you like to use to hit the target.
- Show and tell me which one you prefer and why.
- Choose two different targets. Can you achieve your second target as well as you did with your first target?
- What have you found out?

Teacher considerations

How you interact with individuals, groups and the class will be very different during inquiry-based teaching. Some may find it very straightforward to facilitate while others may find it rather challenging. A point to make here is that inquiry teaching gives ownership to the child. You guide and support, but allow the child enough freedom to explore the task presented. This is different to direct methods whereby you either tell the children how to do it or gradually narrow the activity until the children find the right answer. Inquiry-based teaching is very personal and child centred; therefore, the solutions found to the questions set will be relevant to the child's ability, physique, confidence and creativity. The journey of inquiry and the accumulation of knowledge is as important, if not more, as the execution of the skill. Discussion and further questions may lead to improvements in execution but the premise here is improved understanding which can be retained and transferred to another activity. Your role is different and some conscious planning may be needed, as to what will you consciously be doing while the children are engaged. During inquiry-based teaching the following may need to be considered by the teacher:

- Using a range of equipment may boost inquiring thoughts and creativity.
- I must allow time for inquiry to take place.
- When children are thinking, I do not need to talk.

- Can I ask more questions and give less instructions?
- Elicit answers that belong to the student experience rather than the questions I think are right.
- Share and talk about learning objectives, learning outcomes and success criteria.
- Recognize that learning can be demonstrated physically, orally and in written format.
- Recognize that the academic language required to show understanding has to be part of the sharing of learning objectives and discussion of success criteria process.
- Observe and listen to gather evidence.
- Use questioning and whole class dialogue to check, probe and develop understanding.
- Provide opportunities for children to develop skills in a range of contexts.
- Link skills together to create 'a game': for example, throw a beanbag up and catch, throw a beanbag into a hoop, run around the hoop three times.

Summary

This chapter has explored how physical education is a practical activity. It has considered how such practical activities can also support a range of abilities as well as social, cognitive and practical physical learning. One of the emphases of this chapter has been on your role as a teacher, to ensure that all children are successful and how you would promote success through the facilitation of child success using a blend of open and closed questions. The chapter has also provided ideas and templates that could be used to develop and observe and assess the concepts of inquiry teaching and learning. In this chapter physical education has been shown to have many models that are physical education-specific while also recognizing the many strengths that exist when teaching other curriculum areas. These strengths in your current teaching method can be used and adapted for physical education. This will build your confidence and enjoyment in teaching physical education. Always remember how your physical education lesson needs to include the pivotal learning window as a key to achieving success, progression and achieving learning objectives and how reserve engineering can help you plan. The next chapter will focus on developing physical curiosity and physical development.

Recommended readings

The following three texts are provided as follow-on reading:

1 Hastie, P. (2010). *Student Designed Games*. Champaign, IL: Human Kinetics.

2 Lawrence, J. (2012). *Teaching Primary Physical Education*. Chatswood: SAGE.

3 Pickup, I. and Price, L. (2007). *Teaching Physical Education in the Primary School: A Developmental Approach*. London: Continuum.

Chapter 5
Developing Curiosity and Physical Development

Chapter objectives

- What is physical curiosity?
- How can physical curiosity be fostered?
- What is physical development?
- Fundamental movement skills and physical development.
- Examples of how to plan efficiently and effectively for fundamental movement skills.

Introduction

This chapter will examine how to develop physical curiosity within children's movement and in particular within physical development. Levels and length of time for physical activity have been recommended and set out by the World Health Organization (2010) and NHS (2013) for young children to be physically active for 180 minutes a day of sustained activity for those under 5 years old and for those between 5 and 17 to be physically active at a moderate-to-vigorous level for 60 minutes a day, as being active has health benefits. These can be achieved by getting children moving and being physically active through them exploring their environment and being physically curious as they make sense of the world around them. Therefore it is important to inspire a sense of physical curiosity in our children and to move with them from a young age and throughout their journey through physical education within primary school setting.

This chapter will enable you to begin and evaluate the physical learning opportunities that might inspire curiosity or help the children to develop physically in an educational environment and thus amend and improve practice.

Physical curiosity

Physical curiosity starts at a very early age with infantile responses, in which involuntary movement response to a specific stimulus is seen right from infancy, for example, when an infant holds onto their parents' fingers through the palmar grasp, by grasping their fingers around an object, in this example their parents fingers. Figure 5.1 shows Kaidee has progressed on from the palmar grasp to apply this gripping and grasping technique to be used to hold food steady while eating. The focus for this section is on the movements our young children make, how they understand and see the world through movement. Young children actively explore their own movement capabilities through learning to perform stabilizing, locomotor and manipulative movements. These are often observed first in isolation, and can appear slightly as if the young child is stuttering in their movements, while they make sense of the environment they are in.

Figure 5.1 Grasping and manipulation of food

Almond (2016), from the International Physical Literacy Association, reminds us that for infants, physical curiosity is how they explore and engage in movement, how they learn what their own bodies can do and also how they learn to move in a variety of different directions. The time allowed and needed for exploration is vital for infants to physically learn. This curiosity will be seen in a variety of different ways and a variety of stages from crawling, to falling, to breaking things, to tripping over, to the time when the infants repeat the activity and adapt their movements in response to the previous stimulus and response – it is almost a Pavlovian response when they are so young.

Physical curiosity is often seen in play, especially purposeful play (Almond and Lambden 2016), as the first and most frequently occurring activity in young children. Children within all cultures play and Bruner (1983) described movement and action as representation of the culture of childhood. Most children prefer physical play, and physical competence can be a major factor in influencing social acceptance for all children. Regular physical curiosity can make major contributions to physical, mental and emotional well-being in children. Bee (2000) proposed that children are equipped with motor skills which are like special tools needed for exploring and expanding the environment that helps to support physical development and growth. Smith (2002) suggests that learning through movement occurs for children when there are changes in 'shape and pattern, noise and light along with any contrast'; these are ways to engage their physical curiosity. Figure 5.2 shows Kaidee working through shapes and patterns to put the blocks through the correct holes so they fit within the box. You can tell from her expression that she is totally involved in the movement and working out the problem.

Figure 5.2 Kaidee putting shapes through holes in the box

How can physical curiosity be fostered?

A classic example of how children are curious would be when infants learn to stand on their own feet (quite literally) and they do this without any instruction manual or without fully understanding instructions from adults. Sheets-Johnstone (2013) suggests that children often excel in different forms of movement and Spitz (1983) emphasizes this by proposing that infants' curiosity is stimulated by movement. Within an early years or reception class environment, physical curiosity can be enhanced through the use of sand boxes, water boxes, use of small and large equipment both within the indoor and outdoor environment. As well as providing opportunities for small and large movements through drawing, painting, cutting and use of role play areas, music can also help inspire movement and curiosity which is seen in the way children's bodies move in time or with the music. Within dance situations, exploring ways to move, ways to match movement to the music and to repeat patterns are key for both Early Years Foundation Stage (DfE 2014) and the children within Key Stage 1 (DfE 2013).

Physical curiosity can also be seen through motor development; Gallahue and Ozmun (2006) proposed that motor development is the progressive change in one's movement behaviour that is brought about by the interaction of the individual with the environment and the task. It is affected by hereditary makeup, specific environment conditions and instructions of the movement task itself. Therefore, you can help encourage opportunities for physical curiosity within the indoor and outdoor environments – within the school classroom and physical education or physical development sessions – these will allow for children to have progressive changes and responding to stimulus to allow for interactions with objects, others, environment and task. Also by using and repeating the movement vocabulary that the children are using during their movements and physical curiosity will support their development and understanding of the movement task itself.

Howells (2016) developed and discussed how key vocabulary identified from the Early Years Foundation Stage handbook (DfE 2014) could be used by practitioners to encourage and talk with children while they are exploring and enquiring within their movements (Table 5.1). This can also be used with older children as well as those in reception and Key Stage 1.

Pause for thought – *Thinking about how to record physical curiosity*

Can you make a list of physical behaviours that typify physical curiosity? Could you also ask your colleague to also make such a list and compare your list to your colleague's list?

Can you photograph or video your children showing physical curiosity in floor-based and water-based play?

Table 5.1 Key vocabulary to encourage movement and to foster curiosity (Howells 2016)

Words to describe.......	Example vocabulary
Motion	Stop
	Start
	Forwards
	Backwards
	Sideways
	Space
Actions and ways of moving	Rolling
	Crawling
	Shuffling
	Jumping
	Skipping
	Control
Feelings	Happy
	Sad
	Jolly
	Stormy
	Lonely
	Excited
What happens to the body when exercising	Hot
	Red cheeks
	Breathing more
	Tummy moves
	Sweating
	Tired

For older children in Key Stage 1 and Key Stage 2, more challenges, questions and problem-solving activities can help children foster physical curiosity. Within coordination and control skills in gymnastics, instead of giving direct instructions about how to travel across the mats, rewording of activities will inspire and engage the children. For example: Can you show me ways to cross the mat without using your hands? – this will provide a variety of movements including, but not limited to, walking, skipping, jumping, sliding, shuffling, using bottoms, log rolls, teddy bear rolls, judo rolls. It will make the children consider the direction of travel as well as the body part that is used, and explore ways in which their bodily movements can be successful to complete the answer. Your role within this set up is to help the children describe the movements and directions that have been used to complete the talk and to then set the next challenge, the what next, now that they have been successful.

Coordination and control can also be developed within skills such as through games. For example, if you provide the children with a basketball each and rather than asking them or telling them to dribble, to first ask them to 'explore as many different ways to move with the ball'. Some will immediately dribble the ball with their hands and some with their feet, and some may also produce movements in which their bodies are static but the ball is moving round their bodies; for example, some children bounce the ball between their legs; some children may share ideas even though they do not currently have the ball (Figure 5.3). The next challenge could be linking movements together, moving from a foot and eye coordination movement to a hand and eye coordination movement or linking a static movement of the ball round the body (for example, a figure of the number 8 with the ball between legs) and a dynamic movement (such as walking) so that they are able to move forwards, backwards, sideways while at the same time completing the figure of the number 8. Dischler (2010) supports such teaching ideas as above; within her earlier work she suggested that it was important to encourage children's curiosity by getting children to stop and pause and ponder on difficult questions that have been set. The concept of posing questions allows the children to consider many possibilities that could use small as well as large body movements. It allows children to celebrate their success at the end, as well as consider what they might do, how it might change, thus developing a planning, reviewing, evaluating mindset that we wish to continue into Key Stage 2 and beyond.

Figure 5.3 Children exploring different ways to move with the basketball

What is physical development?

Physical development from a UK perspective was introduced in Chapter 1. The DfE (2014) in the EYFS statutory framework describes it as involving and 'providing opportunities for young children to be active and interactive; and to develop their co-ordination, control, and movement. Children must also be helped to understand the importance of physical activity, and to make healthy choices in relation to food' (p. 8). There are seven areas of learning and development that have been identified within the EYFS (DfE 2014) framework in England. These are communication and language; physical development; personal, social and emotional development; literacy; mathematics; understanding the world; and expressive arts and design. The first three areas listed are also regarded as the 'prime areas' (DfE 2014, p. 7) of learning in which children's curiosity in particular is due to be developed. This is due to the fact that physical development can be used across all the areas of learning as a means for the children to learn.

Within the framework there are early learning goals that physical development sits within: these are early learning goal 4 which is moving and handling and early learning goal 5 which is health and self-care. Within each of these the children have set goals that they are to achieve.

> Moving and handling: **children show good control and co-ordination in large and small movements. They move confidently in a range of ways, safely negotiating space.** They handle equipment and tools effectively, including pencils for writing. Health and self-care: children know the **importance for good health of physical exercise**, and a healthy diet, and talk about ways to keep healthy and safe. They manage their own basic hygiene and personal needs successfully, including dressing and going to the toilet independently. (DfE 2014 p. 10)

The early learning goals show that the emphasis is not just on the physical movements, but also on how the children are able to understand the choice and the decisions they are making. Here are some examples of what exceeding the early learning goals could be, for moving and handling: 'Children can hop confidently and skip in time to music. They can hold paper in position and use their preferred hand for writing, using a correct pencil grip. They are beginning to be able to write on lines and control letter size' (p. 37, DfE 2015). This example of exceeding links forward to the next section on fundamental movement skills and the need to include both fine (small) and gross (large) motor (movement) skills within physical development sessions and physical education lessons to help support and extend these areas of learning. As regards health and self-care the DfE's example of exceeding goals is 'Children know about and can make healthy choices in relation to healthy eating and exercise. They can dress and undress independently, successfully managing fastening buttons or laces' (p. 38, DfE 2015). These kind of skills show the importance of ensuring that there is a time within physical development sessions for putting on and taking off role play clothes that include buttons or laces, and show the importance of developing such life skills when the children get changed in and out of physical education lessons. It reminds us to ensure that time is given for all children to be successful at tying their shoe laces and that they are not too rushed when and if they struggle with this skill, as it is important for them to be able to independently complete this task, and for us to ensure that we give them the opportunities they need to develop this skill.

How physical development benefits children's learning

In Chapter 1 the domains of learning were introduced and discussed (Kirk 1993; Laker 2001) and it was also discussed how physical development could be supported in children's learning. Howells (2015) highlighted the links between the domains of learning to the National Curriculum, below the three domains of learning and now linked to the Early Years Foundation Stage (EYFS) (DfE 2014). The phrases used are from the framework and are then applied to the domains of learning. This can be a way in which you can help support with physical development and the early years physical education lessons. As proposed in Chapter 1 with the Key

Table 5.2 EYFS linked to the domains of learning

Practical	Cognitive	Social
• Controlled effort	• Create moods and talk about feelings	• Confidence
• Active games		• Collaborative throwing, rolling, fetching, receiving
• Energetic play	• Use key vocabulary of movement	
• Use of beanbags, cones, balls and hoops		• Play with one another
• Stand on one foot	• Use key vocabulary of manipulation	• Understand boundaries of self and others
• Move freely		
• Climb	• Pose challenging questions	• Match activity to interests
• Negotiate space, adjust speed, direction, avoid obstacles	• Follow sensible rules	
• Catching, rolling	• Understand how body feels and express how it feels	
• Draw lines and circles	• Know why you get hot	
• Experiment ways of moving		
• Jumping off objects		
• Increasing control over objects		
• Kick		
• Balance		
• Target throwing		

Stage 1 curriculum lesson, plans can be linked to the three domains to help increase awareness and understanding of movement (Table 5.2).

Pause for thought – *Thinking about what do you know already?*

Can you list as many fundamental movement skills as possible?

Can you now group them into categories? What categories did you choose?

Fundamental movement skills and physical development

It is recognized that there are other ways to learn physically and to develop physically as discussed within Chapter 1 such as through physical literacy or through purposeful play (Almond and Alfonso 2014). However, the focus for this section is fundamental movement skills, due to this phrase being used within the National Curriculum (DfE 2013) for Key Stage 1 and the need to ensure that you are confident in teaching and mastering this part of the curriculum. The fundamental movement skills part is included in the first sentence of the Key Stage 1 curriculum; the words in bold are those that link to fundamental movement skills, so it can clearly be seen how this area is the main focus of Key Stage 1 physical education lessons and how children are to develop physically.

- Pupils should develop **fundamental movement skills**, become increasingly competent and confident and access a broad range of opportunities to extend their **agility, balance and coordination**, individually and with others. They should be able to engage in competitive (both against self and against others) and cooperative physical activities, in a range of increasingly challenging situations.

- Pupils should be taught to:
  - master basic movements including **running, jumping, throwing and catching**, as well as developing **balance, agility and coordination**, and begin to **apply** these in a **range of activities**
  - participate in team games, developing simple tactics for attacking and defending
  - perform dances using simple movement patterns (DfE 2013)

Fundamental movement skills are essentially basic skills such as throwing, catching, walking, running and balancing. There are three different categories of fundamental movement skills that are often defined. Gallahue and Donnelly (2003) called the categories locomotion, stability and object manipulation skills and described each category as follows:

- **Locomotor skills**: a change in location of the body relative to a fixed point; moving the body from point A to point B. These can include a variety of different pathways (straight, curved, zig zag). These skills include walking, running, jumping, leaping, hopping, skipping and galloping.

- **Stability skills:** balance both non-locomotor, non-manipulative; involve body stability, balance and most importantly spatial awareness. These skills include twisting, turning, pivoting and performing balances both static and dynamic. These skills do not travel through space but are performed within the child's own personal space.

- **Manipulative skills:** gross and fine motor manipulation; involve the control of objects using various body parts. These can also involve giving or taking an object. These skills include throwing, passing, striking, catching, kicking and receiving objects as well as sewing, and cutting, which links to physical development Early Learning Goals of the EYFS. (DfE 2014)

Examples of the three categories of skills are shown within Table 5.3, adapted from Doherty and Brennan's (2014) work on learning to move and moving to learn.

Many movements involve a combination of stability, locomotor and manipulative movements; for example, skipping using a skipping rope includes

Table 5.3 Three categories of fundamental movement skills

Locomotion skills	Stability skills	Manipulation skills
Walking	Bending/Pointing/Flexing	Handling
Running	Stretching/Extending	Ball rolling/Quoit rolling
Chasing	Twisting	Kicking
Vertical jumping	Turning/Rotating	Throwing
Distance jumping	Reaching	Catching
Jumping (landing on two feet)	Swaying	Trapping
Hopping (landing on the same one foot)	Pushing	Striking
Galloping	Pulling	Punting
Sliding	Swinging	Dribbling
Leaping (landing on one foot, having taken off from the other foot)	Dodging	Volleying
	Rolling	Stopping
Skipping	Balancing	Grasping
Bouncing	Relax and stretch	
Climbing	Static/Stillness	

locomotion (jumping over the rope), manipulation (turning of the rope) and stability (maintaining balance after jumping over the rope, before the next jump). Another example could be playing football which includes locomotion (running and jumping), manipulation (dribbling, passing, kicking and heading) and stability (dodging, reaching, turning, twisting).

Pause for thought – *Thinking of examples:*

Can you take an activity that you do and unpack it in terms of how it is made up of locomotion, stability and manipulation?

What are the parts of the movement that make up each category?

Sometimes the combinations of movements are referred to as fundamental movement patterns, which are the building blocks for more complex skills. For example, a triple jump is made up of a hop, a skip and a jump, that is three locomotor skills joined together to make one movement; however balance and stability are also needed in the skill of stopping. See Figure 5.4 (Pickup and Price, 2007) for the relationship between fundamental and specialized skills. These combination skills (such as discus which includes both the run up and the throw) are due to be taught within Key Stage 1 (DfE 2014) once running, throwing and catching have been developed in isolation; the National Curriculum states that they are also to be combined. There are many more combination skills that can be proposed; for example, javelin throwing is not just about throwing, there is also the run up prior to the throw and the transfer of weight from one side of the body to the other to enhance and extend the throw further through the air. Therefore it is suggested that it is important to understand, plan and develop the fundamental movement skills to ensure children are successful and can develop onto other more complex skills. Miller, as early as in 1978, proposed that for teachers it is the instruction of skill development that is important so that children can understand the movement patterns. You need to provide opportunities for practice and for instruction, to encourage children with positive feedback and reinforcement and to teach each movement in context, for example, throwing for accuracy or throwing for distance.

In teaching movement development, you need to provide opportunities for exploration; this can be time for the children to play, time to experiment. To allow time to discover, this could be a guided discovery situation in which the children can then begin to combine, through practice of their exploration and discovery to put skills together. Here you can observe the children responding and repeating their response to a certain situation or set up. When faced with a similar situation, children will select and apply their skills; here you will see that they are applying tactics to their movement. And then the final stage is refinement, where you will observe that the children have been able to analyse the result of their movements.

Figure 5.4 Pickup and Price's (2007) relationship between fundamental and specialized skills (p. 80)

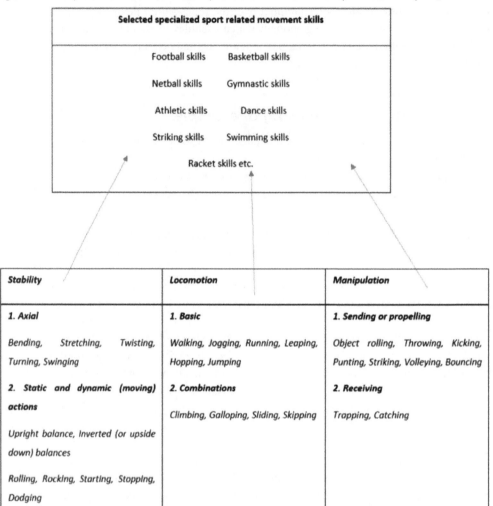

Stability	Locomotion	Manipulation
1. Axial Bending, Stretching, Twisting, Turning, Swinging **2. Static and dynamic (moving) actions** Upright balance, Inverted (or upside down) balances Rolling, Rocking, Starting, Stopping, Dodging	**1. Basic** Walking, Jogging, Running, Leaping, Hopping, Jumping **2. Combinations** Climbing, Galloping, Sliding, Skipping	**1. Sending or propelling** Object rolling, Throwing, Kicking, Punting, Striking, Volleying, Bouncing **2. Receiving** Trapping, Catching

<u>Pause for thought</u> – *Thinking about your learning environments*

How can you use your educational environment to help support children's learning physically?

What opportunities could you set up, both indoors and outdoors, to help foster physical curiosity?

What area do your children use or want to use more? Can you promote this area to encourage physical development or particular fundamental movement skills?

Planning for fundamental movement skills

The Department for Education (2014) offers some support in terms of planning and guiding children's activities and reminds us that there is a need to 'reflect on the different ways that children learn and reflect these in their practice'. They continue and suggest that there are three characteristics of effective teaching and learning which are 'playing and exploring' in which 'children investigate and experience things, and "have a go"'; then there is 'active learning' in which 'children concentrate and keep on trying if they encounter difficulties, and enjoy achievements'; and the third characteristic is that of 'creating and thinking critically' in which 'children have and develop their own ideas, make links between ideas, and develop strategies for doing things' (p. 9). Howells (2015) proposed that there are four core elements to consider when planning, including pace, structure, transferrable skills and competition. Within the lesson plan example, the pace of the lesson is about ensuring that the children are engaged, inspired and excited. The notion that they will just be using a quoit and rolling it may sound easy to some, and yet daunting to others; the posing of questions is key to keeping children motivated. The structure of the lesson is focused on the progression that is occurring within the lesson, how the activities move from one to another, has a sense of flow, a sense of challenge and a sense of achievement. Transferrable skills are skills that are able to be linked to other parts of the curriculum; these will be colour coded or in *italics* in the example and link across to both other elements of the National Curriculum and other fundamental movement skills, such as sending, receiving, trapping, pushing, stopping, timing, confidence, communication, challenge. The purpose of showing the links is for you to be able to use these more in planning, and ultimately in lessons so that it is easier for children to know and to understand how much their skills and activities transfer across their physical movements, physical development sessions and within different physical education lessons. The last part of planning that Howells (2015) proposed is competition. Competition has been previously examined in Chapter 2. However, for the purpose of the example, competition here denotes competition with self and has objective measurements in terms of distance and timings.

Within the example lesson plan (Figures 5.5–5.7) the focus is on quoit rolling as a manipulation category of fundamental movement skills, plus, as the lesson progresses, introducing running and rolling thereby combining locomotor, manipulation and also stability skills. A simple activity such as quoit rolling could be used for Key Stage 1, as it can focus on basic skills in isolation, but this lesson is for Key Stage 2 as it develops the activity from isolation into combination of skills, as per Key Stage 2 National Curriculum requirements (DfE 2013). If you are unfamiliar with what a quoit is, it is essentially a small rubber ring that is the size of a child's/small adult's hand. Otherwise known as rings, these can also be found to be made out of rope or metal and were used in the nineteenth century in a traditional game to attempt to throw onto a peg, where the closest ring to the peg, or those who reached the peg, won. Quoits are often found in primary school physical education cupboards.

> ## Pause for thought – *Thinking about how to plan and encourage travelling (locomotor) movements*
>
> How can you now plan effectively for developing locomotor fundamental movement skills? Can you use the blank lesson plan to help support your own planning?
>
> What would you do to encourage your children to travel or move in a variety of different ways?

Figure 5.5 Example lesson plan part 1

Section of Lesson	Description and Organisation	Teaching Points / questions	Assessment for Learning	
Introduction and Warm Up (Purpose of activity is to get children used to moving the quoit, how it feels and responding to instructions).	Every child to have their own quoit. Start by playing 'Driving in my car', Every child to hold their quoit out in front them as if it was their steering wheel. Explain to the children that on your call that they will move forwards, backwards, (reversing) and on the song lyrics 'driving, driving, I'm driving in my car, beep beep' that the children will take one hand off the steering wheel and pretend to beep their horn. Increase the speed of the car driving, as the activity progresses. (Includes practical domain of learning– controlled effort, active game, moving freely, negotiating space, adjusting speed, avoid obstacles; cognitive domain of learning – key vocab of movement and social domain of learning – confidence and playing with one another)	Drive into space Drive in and out of the other cars Look behind you before reversing / moving backwards. Move your feet faster to speed the car up.	Can the children keep the steering wheel out in front of them with two hands? Can the children keep the steering wheel out in front it the same hand each time or do they change? Do the children drive into space? Do the children look behind before they reverse?	**Commented [K1]:** Fundamental movement skills - Manipulation skills of – handling, grasping and trapping **Commented [K5]:** Transferable skills of Coordination and Control **Commented [K2]:** Fundamental movement skills - Locomotor skills of walking, and then jogging, and then running. **Commented [K3]:** Introducing new vocab **Commented [K4]:** Locomotor skills.
Lesson Activity 1 (Purpose of this activity to find successful way to explore rolling)	Every child to explore how to roll their quoit for a standing position. Allow time for children to explore, use positive language when they are successful, but highlight why. Copy and repeat examples of the different ways to roll, these may be one handed, two handed, between legs, backwards. (Includes practical domain of learning – controlled effort, rolling, adjusting direction and speed; cognitive – answering challenging questions, social – matching activities of others, building confidence)	Can you find 3 different ways to roll a quoit? What are those 3 ways to roll a quoit? Roll into space, look out for others rolling towards you	Can the children roll the quoit? Can the children release it from their hands and roll rather than throw? Can children roll into space?	**Commented [K6]:** Fundamental movement skills – manipulation skills of handling, grasping, rolling. And stability skills of bending, pushing, balancing **Commented [K7]:** These will link to both fundamental movement skills of manipulation and stability. Plus also link to transferable skills coordination, balance and confidence development
Lesson Activity 2 (Purpose of this activity is to find out that the lower to ground the upper body is the easier it is to roll along	Ask the children to all come to the same end of the hall /playground and to get down low to roll the quoit. (Again still give them freedom to explore ways in which to do this) Expect to see sitting, kneeing, lying. Try standing, but with bent knees one foot in front of another, (approximately	What changes to the roll when you're low? Focus on releasing the quoit out of your first finger and little finger.	Can the children get low and roll? Do the children have their feet in opposition to their release hand? Do they have their body facing the direction of	**Commented [K8]:** Fundamental movement skills of manipulation and stability. Plus transferable skills of coordination and balance **Commented [K11]:** Transferable skills – coordination, confidence, cooperative, increasingly challenging.

Figure 5.6 Example lesson plan part 2

the ground)	a step apart), feet in opposition to the hand rolling, roll using one hand, so if rolling with left hand, right foot is forwards and vice versa. Allow the children to watch the quoit roll to where it gets too, and then go and collect. Repeat but extend hand out as if you are being spiderman and shooting out a spider web to the quoit to help with the straight line of the quoit (Includes practical domain of learning – controlled effort, rolling, adjusting direction and speed of the quoit, experiment ways of moving; cognitive – answering challenging questions, social – collaborative use of space, building confidence)	Body facing direction of travel for the quoit. When collecting, look out for other people quoits that may be rolling towards you, move out of the way if they come towards you. Shoot spider webs at your quoit once you have let go	travel of the quoit? Are the children able to pretend they are shooting spider webs? Does the quoit roll in a straight line? Can they move out of the way when a quoit comes towards then?	Commented [K9]: Transferable skill – coordination and balance. Commented [K10]: Fundamental movement skills – stability and manipulation and locomotor. Transferable skills of recognising success, control and balance, using a range of movement patterns. Commented [K12]: Transferable skills of collaboration.
Lesson Activity 3 (Purpose of this activity is to combine both manipulation skills and locomotor skills, can the children run and grasp their quoits)	Rolling and following. For this activity, the children roll as they have been in activity 2 but instead of just watching where the quoit rolls too, lands, then collecting So repeat the activity in 2, but as soon as you have shot spider web at it, you're going to chase after it, and grasp hold of the quoit before it lands. Need to be able to walk / jog / run alongside the quoit and match the speed of the quoit. Repeat but use other hand to grasp, trap the quoit before it lands. Repeat but this time, need to chase after the quoit, turn and grasp the quoit, so need to be able to walk / jog / run alongside the quoit and match the speed of the quoit then adjust speed so go faster, enabling time to turn direction and grasp hold of the quoit before it lands. (Includes practical domain of learning – controlled effort, rolling, adjusting direction and speed to match speed and direction of quoit, active games, energetic play, move freely, experiment ways of moving; cognitive – answering challenging questions, use of movement vocabulary, social – collaborative use of	Need to let go of quoit, spider web it, push of with your balls of your feet and start travelling after. Increase speed by arms and legs moving faster. Change sides of quoit to grasp with other hand Focus on timing of turn and grasp.	Can the children match the speed of the quoit? Can the children match the speed of the quoit and grasp it before it falls on the floor? Can the children match the speed of the quoit and grasp it before it falls on the floor with their other hand? Does the quoit go in a straight line? Do the children push off from the balls of their feet? Can the children turn and grasp?	Commented [K13]: Transferable skills of combination of movements, enjoyment, using a range of movement patterns, comparing performances with previous ones. Fundamental movement skills, of all categories, locomotor, stability and manipulation.

Figure 5.7 Example lesson plan part 3

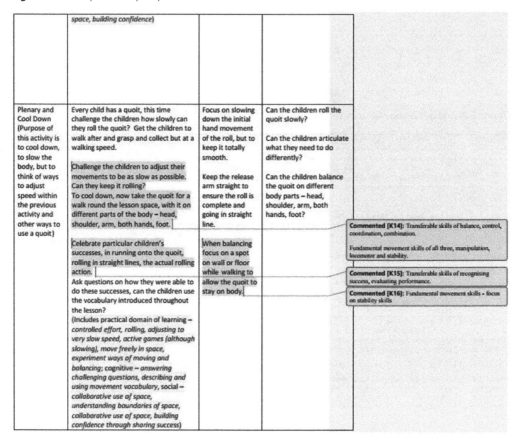

Table 5.4 Blank lesson plan template to aid for future planning

Section of lesson	Description and organization	Teaching points	Assessment for learning
Introduction and Warm-Up			
Lesson Activity 1			
Lesson Activity 2			
Lesson Activity 3			
Plenary and Cool Down			

Summary

This chapter has outlined the importance of physical curiosity that can enhance and develop children's movement and physical development within physical education lessons. It has unpicked and offered suggestions for how physical curiosity could be fostered within the classroom, within the outdoor areas within primary school setting as well as physical education lessons. The chapter has explored what is physical development and how it fits within reception-aged classes as well as Key Stages 1 and 2. It has considered fundamental movement skills and how these skills could be planned for alongside transferable skills linked to the National Curriculum (DfE 2013) as well as the domains of learning. Examples of how all the links can be made were provided within the quoit lesson plan.

The chapter has identified how physical development has a vital contribution to make to children's all round development. Motor and movement skills influence cognitive, social and emotional development (Field 1990). Physical development is an integral part of a holistic approach to child development, in which you have a significant and important role. Your responsibilities include providing frequent opportunities for physical curiosity and physical development to occur throughout the day; to provide positive encouragement; to provide fun activities; to help children to move with control and with the correct movement skills and through the use of key vocabulary describing physical activities that allows children to also communicate their physical activities. The next chapter will consider how to extend, build upon and develop the skills that we discussed in this chapter within physical education lessons.

Recommended reading

The following three texts are provided as follow-on reading:

1 Gallahue, D. L. and Donnelly, F.C. (2003). *Developmental Physical Education for All Children* Vol. 1. Champaign, IL: Human Kinetics.

2 Howells, K. (2015). 'Physical Education Planning'. In K. Sewell (ed.), *Planning the Primary National Curriculum: A Complete Guide for Trainees and Teachers*. Sage: London, pp. 262–76).

3 Doherty, J. and Brennan, P. (2007). *Physical Education and Development 3–11 a Guide for Teachers*. Abingdon, Oxen: Routledge, Taylor and Francis Group.

Chapter 6
Skills to Develop in Physical Education

Chapter objectives

- What skills are involved in physical education?
- What are performing skills?
- What skills should I start with?
- Activity-specific skills that extend children's physical education skills.
- Safety as a skill.
- How to extend and challenge children who are gifted and talented within physical education.

Introduction

This chapter will extend and build upon the concepts of physical development and physical curiosity from the previous chapter and explore the range of skills that children learn and develop within physical education. During the exploration of developing skills, this chapter will consider all ability ranges to ensure high-quality physical education, which is fun, inclusive, inspiring and promotes children's success and progression. It is important to recognize that there may be a range of subject knowledge, expertise and confidence within those teaching primary physical education. Therefore, this chapter will examine how we deliver these skills in relation to the present curriculum (DfE 2013), although it is recognized that these skills help continue to develop children's movement as in the previous chapter and could be applied to curriculum across the world.

Addressing the topics and questions above will enable you to begin to 'unpack' and evaluate your teaching and understand why you choose to use certain skills with your children and why you choose to *develop* certain skills with your children. In doing so, the intention is to stimulate reflection so that we may consider changing some of our practices. A change or improvement in our philosophy or confidence towards physical education, however small, may make a significant impact upon children's experiences, choice and learning within physical education, which will hopefully motivate the children to have a lifetime of better health through improved physical activity.

> ## Pause for thought – *Thinking about how to develop the child wholly.*
>
> Physical education provides a wonderful opportunity to develop holistically. What skills do you want to introduce and develop with your children and most importantly how have you identified these skills?
>
> Are they all physical skills or have you considered social, cognitive and emotional skills as well?

What skills are involved in physical education?

There has been some discussion on skills so far within this book; Jess and Dewar (2004) introduced us, in Chapter 1, to the importance of developing basic skills and movements. Also within Chapter 1 we discussed fine and gross motor skills and how developing these at an early age can help support children's movements by helping them to achieve physical development milestones (Meggit 2006). In this chapter, we consider fundamental skills as well as how through the child's experience of school they will develop a range of skills (all beginning with the letter c!): *competence, confidence, coordination, cooperation, challenge, communicating, collaborating* and *competing* (DfE 2013). The National Curriculum (DfE 2013) also proposes the need of isolated skills to be transformed into combinations of skills, so simple movement patterns become into complex movement patterns. But let us first define what a skill is.

What is skill?

As seen above, the word skill is used in many different ways and there are many definitions of skill, which lead to some agreement in common principles. McNorris (2004) considered the acquisition and performance of skill and proposed that skills tend to be:

- learned
- goal focused – there is an outcome
- specific to a task
- consistent

Taking McNorris's (2004) first idea that all skills are learnt it shows the importance of you as a teacher and your responsibility to help develop movement and skills within your physical education lessons. It is vital to remember that by its very nature physical education should be active and that if children participate in a wide range of activities they will develop a range of physical skills. However, physical education provides us with the opportunity to develop a wide set of skills which are not just physical. For instance, let us look at a selection of the key words taken from the success criteria of the National Curriculum for physical education at Key Stages 1 and 2 (DfE 2013) (Table 6.1); not all of these are physical or practical skills, they also include cognitive and social skills that can be developed through a physical and practical way.

Pause for thought – *Thinking about how to develop cognitive and social skills*

How would you now add into your planning cognitive and social skill development within a physical activity and movement? (See explanation and examples below to help answer.)

Can you add this into your cognitive and social skill vocabulary, into plans, and share it with the children? Try this with a group.

Table 6.1 Application of domains of learning to key skills of National Curriculum

- Being confident (cognitive)
- Being cooperative *(social)*
- Developing linking skills *(practical)*
- Applying knowledge (practical and cognitive)
- Evaluating (practical and cognitive)
- Being competent (cognitive, social and practical)
- Performing a range of skills (cognitive, social and practical)
- Being fair (social and cognitive)
- Developing understanding (cognitive)
- Developing understanding (social and cognitive)
- Communicating (social, cognitive and practical)
- Competing (cognitive and social)
- Collaborating (cognitive and social)
- Knowing how to improve (cognitive)
- Working as an individual (cognitive)
- Giving respect (social)

To explore the above question, we first need to revisit Chapter 1, where the domains of learning were introduced to us and understand how learning in physical education occurs across a range of 'domains' (Kirk 1993). We also need to understand how these domains have been developed and applied to curriculum over the past twenty-five years and will be continued to develop in the future (Laker 2000; Howells 2015). However, the principles are very similar in that the children are learning holistically and they are not just 'playing' within physical education (as seen in Figure 1.12, in Chapter 1). Within the practical domain, when the children are doing and being active, the children are learning not only how to play tag rugby but also how to run forwards, backwards, sidewards, how to move into space, how to hold, send (throw) and receive (catch) the ball. Within the cognitive domain, when the children are thinking, they are learning how to apply and develop skills to link and make actions and sequences, for example, in tag rugby where they learn how to run into a space tactically in the right direction and to be ready to receive the ball. Within the social domain, when the children are interacting and feeling, the children would be communicating to their teammates that they are moving into space, that they do want the ball and that they are ready. The amount of time spent within each of the domain depends upon the learning that is occurring and some activities will require a greater focus on some domains more than others. This will be dependent upon the knowledge, experience and competence of the individual.

From both Table 6.1 and the example above, it is possible to see how as a teacher you could and will apply one or more keywords as a focus for learning. For example, the focus of the lesson may be on 'how to work collaboratively'. The teacher may select a specific activity with set equipment to achieve this. Alternatively, a range of equipment can be used and children are encouraged to choose equipment and create their own activity. The focus in this instance is not the performance itself but how successfully the students collaborated. 'Collaboration' for one group of students may look different to another due to the equipment chosen and the activity that is designed. This situation provides a useful opportunity for children to evaluate their work and to discuss how it can be improved.

What are performing skills?

Locomotor skills: involve moving the body from point A to point B. These skills include walking, running, jumping, leaping, hopping, skipping and galloping

Stability skills: involve body stability and balance. These skills include twisting, turning, pivoting and performing balances

Manipulative skills: involve the control of objects using various body parts. These skills include throwing, passing, striking, catching, kicking and receiving objects

These performing skills have been previously discussed in Chapter 5 (in Table 5.3) linked to early years skills and movement development. They continue within Key Stages 1 and 2. Figure 6.1 illustrates both manipulative skills and stability skills,

Figure 6.1 Manipulative and stability skills

where the child is moving the ball in and out of her legs, showing control of the object of the ball as well as twisting and turning. The example also shows collaborative communication as the child on the right is helping to support the child on the left by also completing the movement, but without the ball.

What skills should I start with?

As a teacher I always ask myself this question to determine what skills I should start with:

'What can my class already do and what else do they need?'

To find the answer to this question we must consider some form of audit or assessment for longer-term planning. This can be set up as a carousel of activities in a multi-skill approach, that is, a variety of skills to be performed from a range of activities. In this way we can see students performing in different ways and then gauge and decide what they can already do and what else they need (Figure 6.2).

There are a wide variety of activities that you may ask your class to demonstrate. The questions within Figure 6.2 are based upon the National Curriculum for physical education (DfE 2013). You can be prescriptive in relation to using a specific piece of equipment or provide a range of equipment for children to choose from. Two circles have been left blank deliberately for you to consider what else may be included. Think about your class and decide what else you will add to the carousel

Figure 6.2 Carousel of activities for Key Stage 2

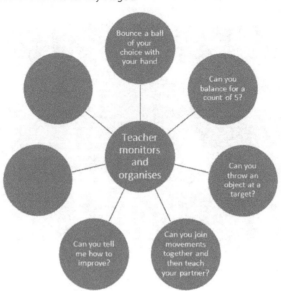

of activities in order to observe how well they can perform and show you what they know and understand. If a carousel of activities seems rather daunting to organize, get all the students to perform one task at the same time and then move onto the next one. Combined with your observations and formative assessment, this can be just as effective.

Table 6.2 shows how we might record your observations in the first few physical education lessons in relation to skill development and the National Curriculum. The table shows which skills are to be observed (adapted from the National Curriculum, DfE 2013) and a list of your children's names. The focus of your observations is: 'Can the skills be performed' or 'applied consistently?' This is an important characteristic of acquiring a skill – it is not a one off. You would shade the box once you can see the skill being used consistently. This may take a more than one lesson and it is okay to take a number of lessons, as this will help you understand what the children within your class are able to do already and where you take them next on their physical education journey. Once you have a completed table, this information can be used as initial formative assessment by you to ascertain the skills that the children have and where the gaps are (a gap analysis) and how they have improved throughout the term or year. This will then provide you with an accurate starting point for planning and setting future lesson objectives and or learning outcomes.

The shading in Table 6.2 identifies the gaps in the children's skills and knowledge. From the shading, it is clear that Ami has really struggled with all of these activities as she has not shown any of these skills. She was not able to complete the skill consistently, which is why these are not yet shaded. She needs specific extra support, while Laura has excelled in all of the skills, as all of them were shaded in the table; she will now

Table 6.2 Example of initial skills audit/assessment

Skills observed *You decide these as the class teacher*	Gloria	Benjamin	Evie	Richard	Alistair	Lewis	Freddie	Harvey	Katie	Laura	Sanjay	Joanne	Susan	Samuel	Chris	Jonny	Anna	Ami
1. Send and receive a ball with their hands or feet																		
2. Send and receive a ball with equipment																		
3. Perform a range of movement patterns and sequences																		
4. Children can tell you how to improve																		
5. Children can work in pairs or groups cooperatively																		
6. Children understand respect and fairness when they compete																		

need further challenges to be set for her. If you consider the whole class, skills 3, 4 and 6 would be our priority for developing next, as these were the least shaded.

So we would start with focusing our lessons on skills linked to:

- Children performing a range of movement patterns and sequences
- Children telling you how to improve
- Children understanding respect and fairness when they compete

The table identifies gaps in capability and can show you where some children can demonstrate all or most of the skills where others cannot. This identification will prove to be useful for you as the teacher to be able to set individual and personal targets. These bespoke targets are useful for assessment for learning and formative assessment which if implemented can ensure effective progress for the child.

What is important to recognize at this point is that the skills identified in the table are quite generic and, for that reason, planning can be really exciting as the skills identified can be applied to a range of activities, from netball to ultimate Frisbee to dance; there are no limitations here. However, the children **MUST** be able to apply them across a range of activities from the curriculum with some degree of consistency which as we discussed earlier is one of the fundamental components of skill (McNorris 2004). The identification of these skills would provide you with an accurate picture of your class and a real time, relevant starting point. This is particularly important if there are limited assessment criteria, as in the National Curriculum (DfE 2013).

You can now decide which activities are best suited for developing the identified skills. If activities within the curriculum are prescribed, that is, netball, then you can still focus on the skills within the chosen activity, all of our identified skills can be done within netball. For help and support in deciding on next skills, look at the core principles of your National Curriculum for physical education for assistance. The skills that you choose are based upon the curriculum and its keywords but you should select those which you deem relevant to your class, year group or Key Stage. Most schools have a range of resources that show how simple skills can be implemented which should give you ideas for tasks and or activities.

Activity-specific skills

Within all schools the subject knowledge of the teacher is finite. Physical education specialists will have detailed knowledge in a range of activities but not all. Teachers who are not physical education specialists **are not expected** to know how to teach all of the activities to a higher level, but they should understand the principles and the skills involved in each activity. It is also important to identify the transferable skills across different activities so the children can see the links and help extend their complex movements. To assist with subject knowledge development, the next section will look at how to apply specific skills to different activities, and these principles should be understood and applied within the curriculum. The activity-specific areas that will be explored are games, gymnastics, dance, athletics and problem-based solving skills in outdoor and adventure activities.

Games

There are many types of games which can be utilized within physical education lessons, some of which are suggested within the National Curriculum (DfE 2013). These are not prescriptive and teachers should provide a wide variety of games for children, which not only reflect our history but also embrace that of other cultures. Bunker and Thorpe (1982, in Griffin and Butler 2005) developed Teaching Games for Understanding, a concept by which children are taught games through playing games (see also Chapter 3) and this approach advocates a thematic approach to teaching games rather than specific individual sports. The idea behind this is that children can see the transferable skills that occur in the categories and can understand the similarities and differences between the different categories (Table 6.3).

Table 6.3 Categories of games

Invasion Games (in which children invade the opposition's area with the focus on a scoring goal)	Striking and Fielding Games (in which children strike an object as far as possible and away from the fielders)	Net/Wall Games (in which children send an object over a net into a space on the opposite side of play and try and prevent the opposition from being able to return the object)	Target Games (in which children send an object towards a specific target and the focus is on accuracy and reaching)
• Football	• Cricket	• Volleyball	• Trigolf
• Hockey	• Rounders	• Sitting volleyball	• Archery
• Lacrosse	• Softball	• Badminton	• New Age Kurling
• Basketball		• Tennis	• Boccia
• Wheelchair basketball		• Wheelchair tennis	
• Rugby			
• Wheelchair rugby			
• Goalball			
• Handball			
• Netball			
• Water polo			

Table 6.4 Generic skills of games

Travelling skills	Sending skills	Receiving skills
With ball	Throwing	Catching
Without the ball	Kicking	Controlling
Look up/forwards	Striking	Positioning to hit
Change of pace	Preparation	Keep eye on object
	Action	Move into line
	Recovery	Withdraw/cushion
	Transfer of weight	
	Keep eye on object	

Table 6.5 Generic principles of games

Attacking	Defending
Creating space	Marking a player
Scoring	Marking a space or zone
Keeping possession	Defending as a pair
All of the above can be developed from individual to pair, group and team skills	Defending as a group

Within games there are **three generic skills** that can be applied to all categories and these can be focused upon within lessons.

Also within games there are also two generic principles that can again be applied to all categories and can be focused upon within lessons

Within gymnastics and dance there are five areas of Laban's analysis of movement (Table 6.6) that can be focused on within lessons. In Table 6.6, questions and teaching prompts have been added to each section, for example, *what is the body doing,* which will help you enable progression of learning through teaching points for development of skills and next steps.

Action words can also be used to help develop skills and movement patterns within dance and gymnastics (Table 6.7). The words can be presented to the children to inspire and challenge them to develop motifs (for dance) and sequences (for gymnastics). You can present them to the children to use as just one category of action words or to combine a mixture of action words from a range of categories. This will help the children progress from simple movement patterns to complex and a range of movement patterns and will link their learning to the National Curriculum for Key Stage 1 and Key Stage 2 (DfE 2013).

Table 6.6 Laban's analysis of movement (Laban 1975)

BODY – WHAT is the body doing?	SPACE – WHERE is the body moving?
PARTS OF BODY	**LEVELS**
Can lead, can support, can relate, can move symmetrically and asymmetrically	High, medium, low
ACTIONS	**DIRECTIONS**
Travelling, stillness, jumping, turning, gesturing, stepping, rolling, sliding, vaulting, twisting, crawling, climbing, running, swinging, balancing, flight, swimming, floating, treading water, striking, fielding, sending, receiving, dodging, chasing, avoiding	Forwards, backwards, sideways, diagonally, high, deep
	AIR and FLOOR PATTERNS
	Straight, curved, twisted, regular
DYNAMICS –HOW is the body moving?	**RELATIONSHIPS** – With whom or with what?
TIME	Alone
Sudden, quick–slow, sustained	Partner
WEIGHT	Small group
Strong, heavy–light, fine	Large group
	Team
	Opponents
	Apparatus
	Equipment

Table 6.7 Examples of action words that could be used in gymnastics/dance

Travel	Rotation	Elevation	Down	Stillness
Whizzing	Spinning	Bouncing	Falling	Freezing
Flashing	Whirling	Bobbing	Drooping	Hovering
Darting	Swirling	Flying	Collapsing	Suspending
Shooting	Twirling	Soaring	Diving	Nestling
Streaking	Tangling	Shooting	Crumpling	Perching
Creeping	Twinning	Swooping	Sliding	Pausing
Plodding	Coiling	Exploding	Subsiding	Slicking
Drifting	Spiralling	Popping	Settling	Gripping
Zooming	Rolling	Pouncing	Melting	Hesitating
Meandering	Winding	Flipping	Sagging	Interrupting
Shuffling	Swerving	Spurting	Sinking	Braking
Gliding	Snaking	Rising	Descending	Hushing
Floating	Orbiting		Cascading	Peacefully
Prancing	Turning		Slumping	Tranquillity
Wondering	Wheeling			Sloth-like

Outdoor adventurous activities

This area provides a wide base to develop a whole range of skills with children. These range from communication and collaboration, to personal challenge through to developing environmental understanding and problem-solving. These types of activities may be offered not only through the use of onsite provision such as outdoor and adventure outdoor playground equipment, but also through residential trips, or visiting local areas.

What do children learn?

- Physical skills – agility, balance and coordination skills as well as specialist movement skills
- Social skills – communication, teamwork, trust and patience
- Cognitive/creative skills – decision making and problem-solving
- Leadership skills – pairs/groups/teams (followers)
- Health and Fitness – activity and knowledge
- Self-esteem – through achievement at all levels
- Confidence – willingness to have a go
- Encourage lifelong participation
- Fun/enjoyment
- A leveller, that is, it provides a different context for children to excel which often leads to different children finding success more than they would in physical education!

Children also learn the idea of planning an activity through completing puzzles or questions. They then review how successful they are and apply their knowledge and understanding (drawn from them solving or struggling with the problem) to try again. This is called the idea of plan, review and redo. It is important to allow children to struggle and make mistakes, to make bad decisions, to reflect and change their mind and try new ways. They do not all have to reach the result that they want the first time.

For children to get the most from outdoor adventure activities it is important that you really know your class, so you can challenge those who have leadership qualities to be given leadership roles within the activities. You should also be aware of who are effective communicators and who needs to develop their communication skills; who has resilience and determination. It is also important that you promote a real ethos of teamwork, instil confidence in children that your learning environment is a safe place, that mistakes can be made and that you will all work together in a team with trust and cooperation. For this you may need to consider further how you group the children (see Chapter 8 for this in further detail). You also need to recognize that outdoor adventure activities can be a vehicle for you as a teacher to develop all these areas to the benefit of their confidence, self-esteem and subsequently achievement

Figure 6.3 Children working as a team

across the curriculum. Figure 6.3 shows children completing a nightline, in which they all follow a trail with their eyes shut/blindfolded and one person who is not blindfolded offers instructions and guidance. The children have to work together socially. The focus of this activity would be on communication, teamwork, trust and patience, as well as leadership skills and confidence to 'have a go'.

Athletics

In Key Stage 1 the athletic skills are very much focused upon in isolation, for example, standing broad jump and in Key Stage 2, the athletic skills are developed from isolation into combination: for example javelin with a run up. The Youth Sport Trust (2005) recommends that for developing running for children with SEND they could be travelling quickly by wheeling, shuffling, stepping or crawling. They propose that visually impaired children may need to run with a partner, each holding onto a quoit (as used in Chapter 5), or a piece of cord. Hearing impaired children

Table 6.8 Three categories of skills within athletics

Running (that are primary age specific)	Jumping	Throwing (these would be lightweight)
100 m	Standing broad jump	Discus
200 m	Long jump	Shot putt
400 m	Triple jump	Hammer
800 m	High jump	Javelin

will need visual signals to support them. As a teacher you need to consider the use of instructions and demonstrations in particular with children with SEND.

Doherty and Brennan (2008) suggested that running could be developed through a variety of ways, they proposed getting children to try pacing themselves in particular over different distances. You can prompt children to think about acceleration and deceleration; particularly important for those in early years is learning how to stop. Other skills recommended include starting and finishing, going round bends and also in straight lines. Again this is important for early years children who struggle, to start with, to run in straight lines. This can be further hindered as the young children can become easily distracted by mums, dads and grandparents cheering them on sports days where the young children end up waving at their family and heading out of their lanes.

For throwing the focus could be on distance, and therefore applied to specific disciplines of throwing such as javelin, or the focus could be on accuracy and therefore could be applied and transferred to other activity areas such as fielding within striking and fielding activities or ball-based games. The Youth Sport Trust (2005) suggests development of throwing skills with children with SEND to encourage them to use chairs or frames to help support their bodies while throwing; to use different types of equipment such as soft balls or bean bags rather than just sticking to the specific equipment for the throw; and also to use and make ramps or gutters to help children send or roll the ball so they can then transfer this throwing/ sending skill to playing Boccia.

As regards jumping, Doherty and Brennan (2008) proposed that jumping could be developed through considering the phases of jumping, including the take-off, flight and landing. As you can see in Figures 6.4 and 6.5, the children are exploring how to take-off. The children are objectively about to measure and record the distance that they are going to jump using cones. They are practising this particular skill in isolation, but would develop this into combinations and move from standing broad jump to triple jump.

In our example school, the children do not have a sand pit, they have to complete standing broad jump and triple jumps without a run up, this means that you can then set them new challenges. For example, they were challenged to complete a standing broad jump that was the same length as their height. This challenge was designed

Figure 6.4 Children practising the take-off

Figure 6.5 Children practising the flight phase

to give the children a marker and objective measure that they could visually see (Figure 6.6), that they then tried to match. They were also told that the current record for make standing broad jump was recorded as 3.73 metre in 2015, so for their height achieving the target should be easily possible! Other challenges that our example school has completed is developing their triple jump skills. The current record for

Figure 6.6 Children measuring the distance in readiness to complete a standing broad jump

triple jump for males is 18.29 metre by Jonathan Edwards and for females is 15.50 metre by Inessa Kravets. The children were asked to estimate how many combined triple jumps (one after the other) they would need to complete to reach the distance of the world records and then complete that number of jumps to see if they reached the distance. The skills developed were not just practical skills, but cognitive as well as social collaboration and competition skills.

Swimming

Within swimming there are several aquatic disciplines that can be considered and linked to our other activity-specific skills. Water polo can be linked to games, synchronized swimming and aquafit can be linked to dance. Swimming can also be linked to some of our 'c' skills that were introduced earlier within this chapter of being able to swim competently and confidently. However, before we can get the children swimming strokes, we need to get the children competent and confident within the water. This is possible through having activities that are fun and game focused, such as having the children in a pool with low depth so that they can touch the floor and then getting them to imagine that they are skiers and they have to ski across to the other side using arms and legs and having shoulders under the water. The focus here is developing arm and leg coordination skills which they will later need as they learn to swim and get used to the whole body being under water. There are many other games that develop confidence too, ranging from games to get their faces wet, to having their faces under the water, to being under the water, to collecting

Table 6.9 Focus areas of skills for swimming (Amateur Swimming Association 2010)

B – body position
L – leg position
A – arm action
B – breathing
T – timing
(Amateur Swimming Association 2010)

objects from the bottom of the pool. These all will build up to enable the children to enjoy being in the water.

The curriculum also proposes that a range of different swimming strokes are developed effectively, for instance, front crawl, backstroke and breaststroke and to be able to perform self-rescue. Differentiating within swimming may appear difficult but it easier than it first seems, for example, to be able to swim 25 metres confidently, you do not have to just keep the children swimming lengths, they can develop skills through building up strength through swimming using aids and support for set times, for example, 30–45 seconds. You could ask them to use a variety of arm and leg actions on their front and on their back to help develop their confidence. The more able swimmers can be challenged by extending the level of complexity in their activities, such as how can they control their breathing to help support their swimming confidently and smoothly on the surface of the water as well as under the water. The skills that are practically developed within swimming are all focused on 'BLABT' (Amateur Swimming Association 2010) (Table 6.9).

Safety as a skill

The gold standard guidance for safe practice in physical education has been produced by the Association for Physical Education (AfPE). Their guidance is produced every four years and is a very relevant and useful resource for ensuring there is safe practice. The umbrella term used by AfPE for all physical activity within an educational setting is Physical Education, School Sport and Physical Activity (PESSPA) (AfPE 2016). Here are some key principles for safe practice, which are reflected within the AfPE guidance (2016). The principles of safe practice are split into two elements: **teaching safely** and **teaching safety** (James and Elbourn 2016, p. 6). It is important to recognize that these two elements are distinct areas and should not be confused. Teaching safely is the responsibility of the teacher to ensure that the activities, tasks, progressions and equipment used are appropriate and safe. Due care and consideration should be given to reducing risk at all times. Teaching safety is a necessary component of learning within physical education. Children should understand about keeping safe within physical education lessons both physically and emotionally. You should be explicit about safety and ensure where appropriate that there are learning objectives delivered which develop children's understanding of why safety is important and relevant to their health and well-being. Teaching children regularly about safety will enable them to improve their decision-making skills on recognizing and managing risk. The acronym **PIE** is used to describe the processes required for safe practice and is explained in the table below on how safe practice can be delivered linked to teaching safely and teaching safety.

Table 6.10 shows the relationship between the components of safe practice. It is clear that preventing harm and informing (giving key information) is the remit of the teacher. Informing and educating is where you can work alongside children to develop knowledge and understanding of safety within physical education and how to respond to different situations. Our role as teachers is to keep children as safe as possible. Physical education lessons should be exciting, challenging, fun and exhilarating, but by their very nature there are risks involved which have the potential to be hazardous and cause accidents. We must recognize that in a class of potentially thirty plus children, each of them cannot be watched over at every moment. Just as important is the ability to develop children's knowledge and understanding of safe practice. To do this effectively you need to have good safety knowledge of the activity and the potential hazards within the space being used. Good teaching and organization are fundamental to keeping children safe. Therefore, we need to reduce or mitigate the risk of injury wherever possible. Risk assessments are a necessary tool to reduce the potential for accidents to occur. Risk assessments should be specific to the school and the spaces used for physical education with them being reviewed on a regular basis. You should be aware of the physical education policy in their school and any other specific requirements to ensure safe practice.

Table 6.10 PIE model, adapted from James and Elbourn (2016, p. 7)

	Preventing Harm	Informing	Educating
Teaching Safely	X	X	
Teaching Safety		X	X

Pause for thought – *Thinking about safety*

Consider the level of understanding children should have so that they and others can be safe in physical education.

What will children be doing in your physical education lesson to demonstrate that they have a greater understanding level and can apply this knowledge while understanding how to be safe and take risks?

It is not possible to cover the multitude of permutations that relate to safe practice. The suggestions here are a starting point for consideration and are not definitive guidance. The AfPE guidance in conjunction with school policies should be used to effectively develop staff and child knowledge and understanding of this area. Below are a set of examples developed to help support safe practice within physical education lessons within primary school and early years' educational settings.

- Teaching should be well organized and planned.
- The space should be checked for hazards (things that are likely to cause an injury) and the equipment for damage or defects. These should not be used and removed.
- Be consistent in the instructions that you give so that children understand the boundaries in which you work.
- Children should be taught how to put out and pack away equipment to understand how to avoid injury, through lifting and lowering correctly, and also so that it does not break and lasts longer which means they get more use from it (not just because it needs putting away).
- Children should be taught to lift and carry equipment safely to build knowledge, understanding and trust within themselves and each other. Once achieved, more challenging equipment can be used which promotes further fun, learning, challenge and progress.
- Children should be encouraged to raise any issues where they feel unsafe in physical education lessons and their findings/issues should be discussed to develop understanding.
- Safety points should be stated clearly and reminders given throughout the lesson where relevant (not as a one off).
- Children should be able to describe how their actions and or those of others are being safe and they should be able to recognize when it is unsafe.
- Where external coaches are used, they need to ensure that they conform to the practices of the school.

Other organizations are involved in safe practice (James and Elbourn 2016), such as the Health and Safety Executive (HSE) and The Royal Society for the Prevention of Accidents (ROSPA). The latter provides additional guidance on appropriate levels of safety and suggests that activities should be 'as safe as necessary, not as safe as possible' (James and Elbourn 2016 p. 59). This is to ensure that children experience increasing levels of challenging activities (DfE 2013). If this does not happen, then children become bored, off task and may disrupt learning. When this happens, there is an increased likelihood for accidents to occur. Therefore, it is vital that there is a balance between the range of challenges provided to children and the level of risk involved. This is discussed further in Chapter 8.

How to challenge and help children who are gifted and talented progress within physical education

Progress and challenge for the most able children within physical education are areas which have been identified as needing improvement by Ofsted (2013). They observed that 'more able pupils were not sufficiently challenged because teachers' expectations of them were too low' (p. 49)

Identification of gifted and talented children in physical education is often a 'hot' or neglected topic. Clear guidance should be provided by schools to ensure that children are identified and supported. To do this, one way would be to use the model created by Morley and Bailey (2006) who have extensively researched this issue. They suggest that the focus should be on the children's abilities within physical education and that we should continue to educate and challenge our most able in physical education lessons. They proposed that there are five abilities that children who are gifted and talented in physical education would excel in (Figure 6.7). According to them, 'Pupils are recognised as Gifted and Talented when they demonstrate high level ability within the full range of PE contexts'(p. 2).

> ### Pause for thought – *Thinking about talented children*
>
> What would the multi-abilities (physical, cognitive, creative, social and personal) for talent look like in your class?
>
> Could you identify a child in your class who may be gifted and talented and how could you tell?

Figure 6.7 Multi-abilities approach to developing talent

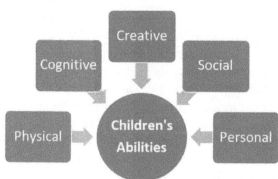

Figure 6.8 Physical ability in Games

That is, gifted and talented pupils excel in one or more of the following abilities:

To explain the abilities in more detail, each of the abilities will be considered so as to understand what they entail.

Physical ability is revealed through children's competence and fitness to perform a range of physical activities. It can be seen through *'excellence in stamina, speed, reaction, flexibility, coordination'* (Morley and Bailey, p. 26) (Figure 6.8).

Personal ability underpins an individual's capacity for self-regulation, self-belief and commitment to mastery. It can be seen through the children setting their own goals and they own achievements. For example, you may ask them to hit a target ten times; this type of personal ability may then be shown by the child adjusting the target so that they hit the target ten times but within a time limit, that is, they stretch themselves by first hitting on the target ten times with the right foot and then again with the left foot.

Cognitive ability is seen in planning movement, completion of problems, tactical movements and composing sequences and motifs (in gymnastics and dance), as well as knowledge and understanding of central physical educational concepts. Children will be able to show this through their understanding and application of transferable skills from one activity to another. For example, they will be able to show that they understand and transfer their sending and receiving skills no matter what the ball size, be it a tennis ball, a ping pong ball, a netball or a basketball or equipment that is different such as New Age Kurling (Figure 6.9). It may also be transferring shape patterns such as pencil/log roll shapes from gymnastics to streamline position in swimming.

Social ability is exhibited in social contexts, and is the basis of leadership, teamwork and similar concepts. It can be seen through 'excellent communication skills and strong leadership skills within a range of environments' (Morley and Bailey, p. 26). The children can often be mistaken as bossy as they will often organize team play and give directions when involved in a game-based situation. Figure 6.10 shows that the boy, second from the right, is a gifted and talented child who is organizing the group and sharing the way in which they should be able to get all of the team over the 'cobweb' and to the other side. He is using his hands within his explanation to try to ensure everyone understands and knows how to work together as a team to be successful.

The last ability is **creative ability** and is evidenced when learners respond to challenges and tasks with fluency, originality and sensitivity to problems. The children can also show this through their understanding and ability of tactics, skills (Morley and Bailey 2006), and also through their use of sophisticated movement vocabulary. Figure 6.11 shows creative ability; the children were asked to 'be on the apparatus, to use no hands be in the widest position you can be in'. Most of the children struggled with this as they could not think about how to be on the apparatus without holding on with their hands. This young girl immediately went to the ladder and demonstrated a wide position with her arms and used her toes to balance so she could be in her widest position.

Figure 6.9 Cognitive ability in adapted activities

Figure 6.10 Social ability within outdoor and adventure activity

Figure 6.11 Creative ability within gymnastics

How to develop transferable skills with children who are gifted and talented within physical education

Children have a whole host of skills that they use in other subjects such as planning, evaluating, presenting and working together. As the teacher it is important that you ensure that these skills are transferred into physical education. Children may then develop these skills in a new context and/or develop new ones. Leadership, organization, communication, officiating and analysis (performing is a given) are additional skills which can easily be developed in physical education. It is essential that children are encouraged to use not only their existing skills within physical education but also their strengths in other subjects. This is difficult to do if you do not take your class for physical education or never watch them as you cannot nurture their skills in other areas. You will have children who are very able and have excellent analysis, leadership, organization, performance and communication skills. Children may have some or all of these qualities to a varying degree. The skill of the teacher is to create opportunities to allow children to exploit their strengths and develop others.

Consideration should be given to how children's gifts and talents can be developed through physical education lessons, after-school clubs, competition, their own sports club (if applicable). There are a wide range of national programmes available to develop talented performers (Youth Sport Trust 2016). It is also important to recognize that there are many opportunities beyond the classroom in terms of enrichment, that is, visits, residential visits, ambassador and/or leadership roles. Children with aptitude for the above should be encouraged not only to participate in other areas of school life for their own development but also to potentially act as a role model for others. Children need to be guided and reminded that many of the skills learnt through physical education and sport have many uses wider than the subject itself.

Pause for thought – *Thinking about how to support gifted and talented children*

Do you have a gifted and talented policy for physical education in your school?

Do you have an updated gifted and talented register?

What provision do you provide for your 'gifted' students in physical education lessons?

What provision do you provide for your 'talented' students in sport?

Do you provide specialist mentoring for your talented students in sport?

Do you fast track 'gifted' students through qualifications, if so what are they? For example, playground leaders.

How do you access CPD for improving your gifted child in physical education and talented child in sport provision?

If you have answered 'No' to any of these questions, please ask your physical education coordinator to support you.

Summary

This chapter has focused on what you need to consider in order to make children safe, successful and have an improved knowledge and understanding of how the progressive use of skills can provide and improve learning in physical education. Through the recognition that learning can be developed through cognitive, social, psychomotor and affective experiences (Laker 2000), you need to ensure that you focus on the needs of the class and individuals and provide curriculum-related learning rather than allowing the curriculum to merely dictate what is to be delivered. The skills section in this chapter provides an overview of the main activities within the National Curriculum (DfE 2013). It is presented in tabular and bullet point form to be easily accessible and to provide useful information that can inform and stimulate your thinking when you are planning lessons and are considering developing skills within activity areas. The importance of safe practice and how it is necessary to provide a safe environment, that is, teaching safely, and also the need to improve knowledge and understanding of being safe, that is, teaching safety (James and Elbourn 2016) were explored. The suggestions within this chapter are provided for the implementation within lessons to the benefit of all children within physical education, including those who are most able. It is important to recognize that physical education has the ability (through the medium of a wide range of activities) to promote learning in a multifaceted way and in doing so provide subject-specific and holistic learning that will develop the child wholly. This in turn can provide a wide range of skills which can be used throughout a person's life. Reflective questions have been used to prompt teacher thought on their own practice and or to promote peer discussion. You should not be anxious about physical education due to lack of subject knowledge, but should use this chapter and book as a springboard to improve knowledge and understanding and in doing so become F.I.T. (FUN INSPIRING TEACHERS)!

Recommended reading

The following three texts are provided as follow-on reading:

1   James, A. and Elbourn, J. (2016). *Safe Practice: In Physical Education, School Sport and Physical Activity*, 9th ed. Leeds: Coachwise.

2   Morley, D. and Bailey, R. (2006). *Meeting the Needs of your Most Able Pupils: Physical Education and Sport* (Meeting the needs of your most able pupils). London: David Fulton Publishers.

3   Doherty, J. and Brennon, P. (2008). *Physical Education and Development 3-11: A Guide for Teachers.* David Fulton Publishers.

Chapter 7
Observing and Assessing Children in Physical Education

Chapter objectives

- How to observe within physical education lessons
- How to assess children while they are learning in physical education
- Explore the three main ways to observe
  - Biomechanical approach to observing
  - Skill phase approach to observing
  - Combined approach to observing
- How to use questions to support learning and assessment

Introduction

This chapter will examine how to observe and assess children while they are learning within physical education lessons. It will explore three main ways of observation; although it is acknowledged that these are not the only ways to observe, these will be the focus within this chapter. Within this chapter we will also consider what to observe, the language that you can use and also how to observe equipment. The second part of the chapter will focus on how to assess the lesson and within the lesson, including the type of questions that can be used to support the children's learning. Examples will be provided throughout the chapter to help you to become more confident in assessing, observing and ensuring progression of all children within your lessons and help improve planning.

Observing

> ### Pause for thought – *Thinking about observing*
>
> What do you look for in children's movement when you are observing within physical education?
>
> How do you observe the movements of ALL of your children within your class?

Within this section three observational approaches will be considered. The first proposed observation is the use of more of a biomechanical approach, focusing on body parts: what the body parts are doing, and what they should be doing! The second is more of a skill phases approach focusing on the use of parts of the skill. The third is a combination of both approaches. For some people they can just 'see' and make observations easily, other people may find the task particularly difficult. Whatever type of 'seer' you are, the purpose of examining these different approaches is to enable everyone to be able to 'see' and to see more clearly. The best way to explain observations is to compare it to game of 'pairs'. For those of you unfamiliar with the card game of 'pairs', it is a very simple children's card game in which you can play individually or you can take turns to turn over cards and the idea is to find two identical objects as quickly as possible. With observing you're essentially trying to compare the movement you're seeing to the equivalent 'pair' on your criteria or listing of how the successful movement should be. Observing human movement is truly exciting as it is all about unpicking how and what has just happened. If what you just observed meets the criteria of the movement then the next step is to challenge and move the performer on, while ensuring that the performer also understands what they just did and to help support their own evaluation and success. It is also one of the most rewarding parts of teaching human movement, physical activity, physical development, physical education and sport.

What to observe?

That is the big question! What to observe? The question may seem more difficult than it needs to be, but there is no need to panic – you will be able to watch all of your class and you will be able to analyse and assess their movements through your observations. When observing it is important where possible to watch the movement all the way through more than once, preferably twice, before making comments and giving feedback, as children are at times sporadic in their movement skills especially at a young age and need time to be able to repeat movements. If you jump in too early and offer suggestions, they may not have mastered the movement yet. Then you as the teacher need to decide – did it look right? Was the movement the same when they repeated it or do you need to watch it again? Do not worry about asking them to repeat the movement for you; children will be excited about showing you again. Was the outcome of the movement – for example, for throwing – what you expected, was it effective? To ensure that children progress you need to give them one thing to focus on. There may be many faults that you have instantly seen or analysed and observed but for them to progress it is about one fault at a time and ensuring the experience is a positive one, so the children wish to progress and move forwards. The key that you need is a set criterion either in your head if you know the particular activity or written down within templates and lesson plans and taken as a checklist to your lessons. Share this with the children at all times; checklist of movements should not be secret; they are excellent tools for self and peer assessment also. With self-assessment the introduction of videos and or photography is needed, which can take time, but can be very beneficial to children's understanding.

Biomechanical approach

The biomechanical approach focuses on body parts, the movement observation template (Table 7.1) can be used to record what happens for one child within the movement. This type of blank sheet would be recommended when you want to record where a child is within their movements. The observation template has five boxes, the first to record the movement that is being recorded, which is key to refer back to when the later observation is also recorded. The rest of the boxes are related to body parts. The template can also be extended to link six parts of the body, if you wish to separate out arms and hands and also legs and feet.

An adaptation can be made to the movement observation template to have it as a comparison sheet, so as to have the recorded movements on one side and the actual teaching points/techniques of the movement on the right-hand side to be used as comparison. This can also be used by the children themselves so that they can evaluate their own and others' performances as per the National Curriculum (DfE 2013). The parts of the movements skills or the parts of the body can be used by you to support what the next positive challenges will be plus help children identify what they are seeing and what the teaching points are to support successes as well as the next steps.

The movement within the example on the next page is of a basic rotation. The rotation itself – a sausage/pencil/log roll – actually entails the same physical movement, but is just referred to in different terminology dependent on which physical education lesson plan text you read.

The following figures 7.1–7.5 show Joseph completing a log roll and Table 7.3 shows how the template links to the figures. The recording of the movement on the left hand of the template has been completed in italics, so it is possible to see what Joseph is doing compared to the teaching points of the log roll.

Figure 7.1 Joseph starting on his tummy for the log roll

Figure 7.2 Joseph turning onto his back

Figure 7.3 Joseph at mid-turn point as he moves from his back to his tummy again

Figure 7.4 Joseph in the later turn phase

Figure 7.5 Joseph completing the log roll

Following the observation, the next step I would do is to ask Joseph this question: 'Tell me something about your head, body, arms and legs, what did you notice, what did you like, what made you get stuck and have lots of giggles on your back?' This would promote evaluation and analysis skills even at this young age and also recognize that enjoyment is part of the movement. Then the next progressive steps of focusing on his legs and arms in particular would be recommended and feedback for Joseph would be provided which would help his whole rotation within the log roll; first suggestion for him would be to have his legs together throughout the movement and then for his arms to start and stay above his head by his ears. His arms in particular will help him start the movement and not get him stuck as his shoulders are in the way, even though this provided lots of giggles. Having his legs together will allow the momentum that he generates at the start of the rotation to continue throughout the whole movement. The key is to offer one observation at a time to allow him to have another go and then focus on the next progression; this will help support Joseph in his next steps of movement development and boost his confidence to try the task again.

The final adaptation that can be made from using the same movement observation template is to be used as a tick list for a group or class of children (Table 7.4). Within the following example the use of ticks and crosses indicate what has been achieved or not. There are also small comments that are included within the observation boxes that indicate part of the movement that was achieved successfully or where the child was struggling with the particular movement. These particular areas would have been the direct focus for input, feedback and positive challenges. Where a child, for

Table 7.1 Blank template of movement analysis template

Movement observation template
Movement Being Observed:
Head
Arms/Hands
Body
Legs/Feet

Table 7.2 Movement observation template used as a comparison template

Movement observation comparison template	
Movement Being Observed: Log/Sausage/Pencil Roll	
Head	**Head** Off the mat, chin tucked towards chest, does not have to be fully on chest. Keep head off the mat as rotate. No use of forehead to help the roll over!
Arms/Hands	**Arms/Hands** Straight along the side body, above the floor pointing towards walls (not ceiling), arms in dish shape to start. Form into arch shape as you rotate, then back into dish shape at end. Hands and, in particular, fingers to be off the floor/mat. Elbows to be up and off the floor/mat to help support the dish and arch positions.
Body	**Body** Starts at the edge of the mat, lying on back. Body forms a dish shape to start with, and as the body rotates onto the front, it forms an arch shape. Good core stability is needed and rotation is controlled throughout the middle of the movement using the core. Body helps to keep the momentum going throughout the rotation.
Legs/Feet	**Legs/Feet** Legs to be used up and across the body to help the start of momentum. Legs and feet up to form a dish shape, then an arch, then dish shape as the body rotates. Toes pointed Feet off the floor at all times (no toes, helping to move the body over).

Table 7.3 Completed movement comparison template with Joseph's movements in italics

Movement observation comparison template	
Movement being Observed: Log/Sausage/Pencil Roll	
Head *Starts with head off the mat while on time, looking up towards the sofa.* *Unable to keep head off mat while rotating, puts head down on the floor.* *Head stays on floor, while he has a mini rest on his back; he giggles.* *Uses head to rotate on the side of his head.* *Lifts head back up for finish position and has chin tucked same as starting position.*	**Head** Off the mat, chin tucked towards chest, does not have to be fully on chest. Keep head off the mat as rotate. No use of forehead to help the roll over!
Arms/Hands *Arms not above head, arms and hands used to push self of the floor from tummy.* *Hands out to the side while on back.* *Elbows used to help turn body over.* *Hands used to balance as he turns from back onto tummy.* *Forearms used to balance at the end of the rotation.*	**Arms/Hands** Straight along the side body, above the floor pointing towards walls (not ceiling), arms in dish shape to start. Form into arch shape as you rotate, then back into dish shape at end. Hands and in particular fingers to be off the floor/mat. Elbows to be up and off the floor/mat to help support the dish and arch positions.
Body *Started lying on tummy.* *Body not in dish shape, or arch shape.* *Rotation is led by the legs in first part of the movement until back is reached; then arms lead, then the legs, causing the body to be a bit 'wonky'.* *Many giggles in the middle of the rotation, core stability working within giggles.*	**Body** Starts at the edge of the mat, lying on back. Body forms a dish shape to start with, and as the body rotates onto the front, it forms an arch shape. Good core stability is needed and rotation is controlled throughout the middle of the movement using the core. Body helps to keep the momentum going throughout the rotation.
Legs/Feet *Legs lead the movement, this helps start the momentum.* *Legs go into a star shape when he rotates onto back.* *Knees used to help rotate from back onto tummy.* *Legs quite wide apart.* *Toes pointed through most stages of the rotation.* *Feet off the floor at the end position of the rotation.*	**Legs/Feet** Legs to be used up and across the body to help the start of momentum. Legs and feet up to form a dish shape, then an arch, then dish shape as body rotates. Toes pointed. Feet off the floor at all times (no toes, helping to move the body over).

Table 7.4 Movement observation tick-list template used for group

Movement observation tick-list template						
Movement Being Observed: Log/Sausage/Pencil Roll						
Head	Eleanor	Amelia	Gloria	Freddie	Jonny	Billie
Off mat, chin tucked towards chest, does not have to be fully on chest.	✓	✓ (at start)	✓	✓	✓	✓
Keep head off the mat as rotate.	✓	✗	✓	✓	✓	✓
No use of forehead to help the roll over!	✓	✗	✓	✓	✓	✓
Arms/Hands						
Straight along the side body, above the floor pointing towards walls (not ceiling), arms in dish shape to start with.	✓	✓	✓	✓	✓	✓
Form into arch shape as child rotates, then back into dish shape at end.	✓	✗	✓	✓	✗	✗
Hands and, in particular, fingers to be off the floor/mat.	✓	✗	✗ (fingers helping over)	✓	✗	✗
Elbows to be up and off the floor/mat to help support the dish and arch positions.	✓	✗	✓	✗ (elbows pushing over)	✗	✗
Body						
Starts at the edge of the mat, lying on back.	✓	✓	✓	✓	✓	✓
Body forms a dish shape to start, as child rotates onto front, body forms an arch shape.	✓	✗	✓	✓ (struggle holding arch shape)	✓	✓
Good core stability is needed and rotation is controlled throughout the middle of the movement using the core.	✓	✓	✗	✗	✓	✓
Body helps to keep the momentum going throughout the rotation.	✓	✓ (almost too fast)	✓	✓	✓	✓
Legs/Feet						
Legs to be used up and across the body to help the start of momentum.	✓	✓	✓	✓	✓	✓
Legs and feet up to form a dish shape and then an arch, then dish shape as body rotates.	✓	✗	✗	✗	✓	✓
Toes pointed.	✗	✓	✗	✓	✓	✓
Feet off the floor at all times (no toes helping to move the body over).	✓	✗	✗	✓	✓	✓

example, Eleanor, has almost mastered this rotation, her next steps would be focused on speed or direction or pathways, or combining this rotation with another movement to form a sequence. There is always a next step, and with gymnastics the easiest next steps focusing on the same movement to ensure that it is repeated, developed and mastered are:

1 To change the speed of the rotation, this would introduce more body control to slow the whole movement down; slowing is harder than speeding up. When asking the children to speed up the movement the focus should be on how to stop at the end of the movement, so it is safe and complete.

2 To change the direction of the rotation such that the body starts with the head and feet at opposite end; so instead of the right side of the body being next to the edge of the mat, the left side of the body would be next to the edge of the mat, the child would then have to consider how to move the 'new' lead leg.

3 To change the pathway of the rotation, this can be done in a variety of ways, by changing the starting position, so the child starts the rotation on their stomach rather than their back or the pathway is now tummy, back, tummy instead of previously being back, tummy, back for a full rotation.

4 To consider how to get into the rotation – how to enter, how to exit, can another movement be added to the beginning and finish – thereby developing a sequence but still focusing on the rotation they have just mastered.

Skill phases analysis approach

The skills phases analysis approach looks at the fact that most skills can be divided into three phases:

1 The preparation phase

2 The action phase (or sometimes referred to as the execution phase)

3 The recovery phase

The three phases are essentially the beginning, the middle and the end of the movement, technique or skill. The best way of understanding the phases is the preparation phase – it is everything the child needs to do before their body moves into position to the movement. The preparation phase may also include preparing equipment such as a racket/stick to be in the right position to be ready to complete the movement. The action phase is all the movements that are required to complete the movement (the action) and then the recovery phase is how to get back into position or to regain balance at the end of the movement; this can be as simple as putting arms behind their body.

The below example shows how it can be used for unpicking and observing a forward roll.

Table 7.5 Blank template for skill phases approach

Skill phases observation template		
Skill being Observed:		
Preparation Phase	**Action Phase**	**Recovery Phase**

Table 7.6 Skill phases observation template with forward roll as an example

Skill phases observation template		
Skill Being Observed: Forward Roll		
Preparation Phase	**Action Phase**	**Recovery Phase**
Start in standing position, arms up, body straight, like a pencil, then crouch down in readiness of the rotation	Pushing off from balls of feet, feet come off the floor	Push up off balls of feet and hands to regain standing position
Feet on the Mat	Pushing off from hands, hands come off the floor	Arms go up straight and into the air
Knees bent	Pushing hand and feet at same time	Looking forward
Hands should be wide apart	Landing and rolling across back, down the spine, in a forward direction	Returning to original straight pencil shape
Head tucked in, chin close to chest	No neck or head involved in action phase	
Bottom up, imagining looking between knees through and up towards the lights/ceiling	Feet and hand touch the floor again	

Emma is demonstrating a forward roll for us and the observation template has been highlighted in bold with what can be seen within the Figure 7.6. On the left of the photograph Emma is in the preparation phase, in the middle of the figure Emma is in the action phase and the right-hand side shows Emma in the recovery phase. The figure does not show Emma getting down into the crouched position just before the action phase, so this explains why these are not highlighted in the completed Table 7.7. Within the action phase the figure has highlighted that she is

Figure 7.6 Emma in the preparation, action and recovery phases of a forward roll

Table 7.7 Completed skills observation template for Emily's forward roll

Skill phases observation template		
Skill Being Observed: Forward Roll		
Preparation Phase	**Action Phase**	**Recovery Phase**
Start in standing position, arms up, body straight, like a pencil, then crouch down in readiness of the rotation	**Pushing off from balls of feet, feet come off the floor**	**Push up off balls of feet and hands to regain standing position**
Feet on the Mat	**Pushing off from hands, hands come off the floor**	Arms go up straight and into the air
Knees bent	**Pushing hand and feet at same time.**	**Looking forward**
Hands should be wide apart	Landing and rolling across back, down the spine, in a forward direction	Returning to original straight pencil shape
Head tucked in, chin close to chest	No neck or head involved in action phase	
Bottom up, imagining looking between knees through and up towards the lights/ceiling	Feet and hand touch the floor again	

using her head within the action of the forward roll; this is key and the immediate feedback for Emma was *to roll on her back*, and she was directed to the right part of the body to rotate onto. The recovery phase shows that Emma has very quickly come off her feet and is heading to return to standing. Her momentum and use of hands to push herself back up to the original straight pencil shape is very clear. However, with the skills phases and using photographs there is a need for more photographs to be able to capture all parts of the skill phases. This is particularly important when using the photography with children to help develop either self-assessment or evaluation and analysis skills, so they do not feel they are doing things wrong, when actually it is just that some actions are just missed out when the photographs are taken.

Biomechanical and skill phases analysis approach

The biomechanical and skill phases approach essentially combines both of the templates into one so each part of the movement, each phrase of the skill has a focus of the body part (Table 7.8). The use of the templates can really help in particular upper Key Stage 2 children to understand, know and evaluate their performances and understand how to improve (DfE 2013).

Table 7.9 is an example of how a forward roll can be observed using the biomechanical and skill phases observation template.

Table 7.8 Blank template for biomechanical and skill phases approach

Biomechanical and skill phases observation template		
Skill Being Observed:		
Preparation Phase	**Action Phase**	**Recovery Phase**
Head	Head	Head
Arms/Hands	Arms/Hands	Arms/Hands
Body	Body	Body
Legs/Feet	Legs/Feet	Legs/Feet

Table 7.9 Example of forward roll within the biomechanical and skill phases observation template

Biomechanical and skill acquisition observation template		
Skill Being Observed:		
Preparation Phase	**Action Phase**	**Recovery Phase**
Head	**Head**	**Head**
Face forwards to start, then when you go into crouch position, tuck chin close to chest, imagine looking through knees up and towards the lights/ceilings	No neck or head involved in the rotation movement Head kept tucked at all times of the action phase	Looking forward, return to original pencil shape
Arms/Hands	**Arms/Hands**	**Arms/Hands**
Start with standing straight up to form pencil shape When you go into crouch position, hands go onto the mat, shoulder width apart	Push off hands (at the same time as you push off from balls of feet) Hands come off the floor Hands return to the floor after the back rotation	Push off hands to regain standing position Arms go straight up into the air
Body	**Body**	**Body**
Body straight at start Then crouch down in readiness to rotate, small-sized body position Bottom comes up in crouch position	Land onto back and rotate across back (down the spine, in a forwards direction)	Body comes out of crouch position to become straight as at the start of the movement
Legs/Feet	**Legs/Feet**	**Legs/Feet**
Feet on mat When moving to the crouch position, bend knees	Push off from balls of feet (at same time as push off from hands) Feet come off the floor Feet return to the floor after the back rotation	Push up off balls of feet to regain standing position

Consideration of language, application of approaches

All too often in physical education lessons, there is the positive praise sandwich, the phrasing of which is something like this: 'Jonny that was a lovely cartwheel, but your legs weren't very high, you need legs to be higher.'

A positive word to boost the self-esteem and confidence can have quite an impact on our young children and vice versa; in this case it could be done by taking a moment and focusing purely on what was actually lovely about Jonny's cartwheel. Your suggestions need more details that the child can follow, otherwise children will switch off, that is, they will only register the lovely comments and nothing said beyond that. The details therefore need to include information on how Jonny can actually get his legs higher. He probably knows he needs to get his legs higher, but you're the significant other, you're the one who is supposed to be giving him the guidance to help him. Therefore, the author suggests, as per the National Curriculum (DfE 2013), that the teacher provide more positive challenges and more explanation of why and how the suggestions will work to aid the children's ability to evaluate and analyse their own successes. It would, therefore, be recommended that a phrase like this is used:

> Jonny that was a lovely cartwheel as I could see you using your hands to take your body weight as you kicked your legs up. Your next challenge is for your feet to try and reach the ceiling, by kicking harder as you kick up and into the cartwheel.

This way Jonny is fully aware that he has nailed the weight-onto-his-hands part of the cartwheel; now he has an aim of getting his feet towards the ceiling, so he has to focus to reach up high and he knows how to do it – by kicking harder. He can then set off and try your challenge while you see another child within the class. This gives you a reason to revisit Jonny later within the activity. With this example of Jonny I have used two of the approaches: the body parts observation in which my focus is on what his hands and legs are doing. The second approach is skills observation in which the focus is on what is happening during the action phase (the 'doing' part of the movement/skill) of the observation.

Figure 7.7 Heath completing a cartwheel

If you look at Figure 7.7 of Heath completing his cartwheel you can see that the key is his left hand. At the moment his left hand is not flat, it is not in the same direction as his right hand, you can see this from the direction of the fingers, and it is a little wide apart, so his shoulders are not in line. If he were to plant his left hand flatter on the mat, this will help him feel more confident in being able to hold his body weight through his hands when he kicks up. If his right arm is firmly planted by bringing his left hand in a little more so that it is under his shoulder, this will help with the transfer of weight and then this will help with the second part of the kick within the action phase. His next progression and positive challenge would be: 'Heath, I want you to focus on your left hand when you complete your next cartwheel and try to have to totally flat on the mat so you can use it to push on in the same way that you are using your right hand.'

After he has achieved this, I would then focus on the orientation of the hand, then the shoulder width. Each step is small, but would make great improvements in the overall movement and confidence and enjoyment of physical education for Heath.

Observing equipment

> ### Pause for thought – *Thinking about observing equipment!*
>
> What does observing equipment mean to you?
>
> Have you observed equipment rather than children before?
>
> When would you observe equipment and not children?

There are many 'secrets' to observing and it is not about being overwhelmed for having to keep an eye and observe every child when the entire class is on the move, but it is about looking out for signs and signals in the way children play without having to watch the actual movement in the activity. For example, when teaching to throw a javelin, you do not need to have watched the children throw the javelin, you can actually observe and comment on your whole class just by watching where the javelin lands. It is enough to have observed the flight path of the javelin or the landing position of the javelin to be able to know what happened with the movement AND to be able to give feedback, especially if the setting in which you are teaching javelin is a non-windy day (Figure 7.8).

If a javelin is released straight and with the hand and arm forward it will land in a position that is almost like a straight line in front of the child. If the child is right handed and the javelin has landed to the left of the child then the child has released the javelin too late, and has crossed that body with their arm. This is the case in the

Figure 7.8 Javelin landing positions

photograph for javelin labelled A and labelled B. Your positive suggestion for the child here could be: 'Your challenge is to release the javelin earlier, your arm is to wave goodbye to the javelin, this will help stop the continued cross, across the body.'

If the javelin of the right-handed child is to the right of the child when it landed, then the child has released the javelin too early and possibly has not fully extended their arm prior to release; this is the case in the photograph for the javelin labelled C. What positive challenge would you provide for the child next? If the javelin lands close to the child but in a straight line, the child has released the javelin too late and they have held onto the javelin past the optimum release point. You can encourage the child to look for a spot on further along the field/playground, you can even put a spot or a cone down for them and get them to imagine they are pointed further down the throwing area; this will help them release with their hand further up in the air allowing for the javelin to float and fly further through the air. The opposite is true of the left-handed child. So if the children are left-handed then A and B are the javelins that they have released a little early and possibly they have not fully extended their arm prior to release, while javelin C is the javelin that was released a little late. For you to effectively observe and provide feedback based on the status of the equipment, you need to know who threw which javelin and which is the dominant hand of the child you are commenting on.

Observing end of movements

Another secret to observing whole class movements to help support children is to be aware of the starting position of the child, but to focus on the end positions, that is, where they are finishing. For example, if Gloria is completing a backward roll across a mat and she starts in the middle of the mat at one end but finishes at the side of the mat, it is clear from this observation that she has travelled diagonally or at least towards one side. This would indicate that she didn't push herself over in the backward roll equally of both hands and that is more than likely when she went for her 'biggest press up in the world'. She did not do this evenly, she actually pushed harder with one hand than the other; the direction that she landed would indicate the side in which she pushed harder on. Her positive challenge could then be: 'Gloria on your next backward roll, I want you to focus on your left hand and push push push with this one as well as your right hand to allow you to finish in the middle of the mat.'

Again your feedback should be focused on direction and how to move forward and challenge should explain what to do next.

Figure 7.9 shows Jessica's end point from her forward roll. She is balanced; she has completed the roll and is in the process of standing up. However, before reading on, think on how is she getting up, what part of her body is she using to get up? Is it her hands? Is it her feet? Is it her legs? Is it something else? Can you use the head, body, arms and legs format to identify what she is doing?

She is actually using her knees; by squishing and pushing them together they are helping her balance and stand up. You can tell this by the way she has her feet turned in and the side of her feet almost off the floor, and the angle of her lower legs. She is

Figure 7.9 Jessica's finishing position

also focusing on the floor which is making her a little wobbly as she stands up. The next positive challenge for her would be: 'Jessica on your next forward roll, I want you to focus on pushing down through the balls of your feet as you stand up and to look more forwards towards the wall.'

This allows Jessica to focus on a body part that will make a difference in her balance, and at a particular point, the end point of the movement.

Assessment

Assessment follows on from observation, it can be the same thing. What are you observing, what are you assessing within the movement, within the skill, within the tactic, within the learning that you want to record to help the children progress and move forward. Howells (2015) proposed that the key to assessment was to ensure that it has clear objective measurements such as time, distance and weight and that the focus is on the children's performance and their improvement and not necessarily on who is the best. For example (Table 7.10) if Neil has only ever jumped 1 metre within the standing broad jump, and Rich has jumped 1 metre 25 centimetres, then our comparison of the two boys' performance shows that Rich jumps the farthest. However, if we focus on the next time that they both jump, where Neil jumps 1 metre 10 centimetres and Rich jumps 1 metre 27 centimetres, here Rich again is still the farthest jumper, but Neil has improved significantly more. It is important to be able to keep records of assessment of this type of objective measurement, so Neil can be motivated and inspired to continue to excel in his own personal achievements. They also need to be celebrated.

Other ways of assessing can be through the questions that you ask yourself about the movements. For example, in Chapter 5 we looked at the quoit rolling lesson. The questions under the assessment for learning box were all linked to teaching points within the lesson or to the description of the activity – in simple 'can they?' phrases. Many people wish to make physical education seem much more complicated than it needs to be. The key is to be able to assess the learning that is occurring within the lessons, and to be able to plan for these effectively, you need to give yourself prompts that are linked to the teaching points and observations that you will be making, so your assessments are objective and measureable. Each of the questions within the below example are yes or no questions that link to the teaching points; so if the

Table 7.10 Recording for standing broad jump

Name of child	Jump one	Jump two	Difference
Rich	1 m 25 cms	1 m 27 cms	2 cms
Neil	1 m	1 m 10 cms	10 cms

Table 7.11 Example lesson plan with focus on quoit rolling

Section of lesson	Description and organization	Teaching points/questions	Assessment for learning
Introduction and Warm-Up (Purpose of activity is to get children used to moving the quoit, how it feels and responding to instructions)	Every child to have their own quoit. Start by playing 'Driving in my car'. Every child to hold their quoit out in front them as if it was their steering wheel. Explain to the children that on your call they will move forwards, backwards (reversing), and on the song lyrics 'driving, driving, I'm driving in my car, beep beep' that the children will take one hand off the steering wheel and pretend to beep their horn. Increase the speed of the car driving, as the activity progresses	Drive into space Drive in and out of the other cars Look behind you before reversing/ moving backwards Move your feet faster to speed the car up	Can the children keep the steering wheel out in front of them with two hands? Can the children keep the steering wheel out in front of them with one hand, is it the same hand each time or do they change? Do the children drive into space? Do the children look behind before they reverse?
Lesson Activity 1 (Purpose of this activity is to find successful ways to explore rolling)	Every child to explore how to roll their quoit for a standing position Allow time for children to explore; use positive language when they are successful, but highlight why Copy and repeat examples of the different ways to roll, these may be one handed, two handed, between legs, backwards	Can you find three different ways to roll a quoit? What are those three ways to roll a quoit? Roll into space, look out for others rolling towards you.	Can the children roll the quoit? Can the children release it from their hands and roll rather than throw? Can children roll into space?

Lesson Activity 2 (Purpose of this activity is to find out if it is easier to roll along the ground when the upper body is lower to ground)	Ask the children to all come to the same end of the hall/playground and to get down low to roll the quoit. (Again give them freedom to explore ways in which to do this) Expect to see sitting, kneeling, lying Try standing, but with bent knees, one foot in front of another, (approximately a step apart), feet in opposition to the hand rolling, roll using one hand, so if rolling with left hand, right foot is forwards and vice versa. Allow the children to watch where the quoit roll gets to, and then go and collect Repeat but extend hand out as if you are being Spiderman and shooting out a spider web to help with the straight line of the quoit	What changes to the rolling action when you're low down? Focus on releasing the quoit out of your first finger and little finger Body facing direction of travel for the quoit When collecting, look out for other people quoits that may be rolling towards you, move out of the way if they come towards you Shoot spider webs at your quoit once you have let go	Can the children get low and roll? Do the children have their feet in opposition to their release hand? Do they have their body facing the direction of travel of the quoit? Are the children able to pretend that they are shooting spider webs? Does the quoit roll in a straight line? Can they move out of the way when a quoit comes towards them?
Lesson Activity 3 (Purpose of this activity is to combine both manipulation skills and locomotor skills, to find out if the children can run and grasp their quoits)	Rolling and following. For this activity, the children roll as they have been doing in activity 2 but instead of just watching where the quoit rolls to, lands, they also collect it So repeat the activity in 2, but as soon as you have shot spider web at it, you're going to chase after it, and grasp hold of the quoit before it lands. You need to be able to walk/jog/run alongside the quoit and match the speed of the quoit	Let go of quoit, spider web it, push it off with the balls of your feet and start travelling after Increase speed by arms and legs moving faster Change sides of quoit to grasp with other hand Focus on timing of turn and grasp	Can the children match the speed of the quoit? Can the children match the speed of the quoit and grasp it before it falls on the floor? Can the children match the speed of the quoit and grasp it before it falls on the floor with their other hand?

(Continued)

Table 7.11 (Continued)

Section of lesson	Description and organization	Teaching points/questions	Assessment for learning
	Repeat, but use other hand to grasp, trap the quoit before it lands		Does the quoit go in a straight line?
			Do the children push off from the balls of their feet?
	Repeat, but this time, need to chase after the quoit, turn and grasp the quoit, so you need to be able to walk/jog/run alongside the quoit and match the speed of the quoit; then adjust speed to go faster, providing time to turn direction and grasp hold of the quoit before it lands		Can the children turn and grasp?
Plenary and Cool Down (Purpose of this activity is to cool down, to slow the body, but to think of ways to adjust speed within the previous activity and other ways to use a quoit)	Every child has a quoit, this time challenge the children how slowly can they roll the quoit? Get the children to walk after and grasp and collect it but at walking speed	Focus on slowing down the initial hand movement of the roll, but to keep it totally smooth	Can the children roll the quoit slowly?
	Challenge the children to adjust their movements to be as slow as possible. Can they keep it rolling?	Keep the release arm straight to ensure the roll is complete and going in straight line	Can the children articulate what they need to do differently?
	To cool down take the quoit for a walk round the lesson space, balancing it on different parts of the body – head, shoulder, arm, both hands, foot	When balancing, focus on a spot on wall or floor while walking to allow the quoit to stay on body	Can the children balance the quoit on different body parts – head, shoulder, arm, both hands, foot?
	Celebrate particular children's successes, in running onto the quoit, rolling in straight lines, the actual rolling action		
	Ask questions on how they were able to do these successes, can the children use the vocabulary introduced throughout the lesson?		

answer is no at all, I immediately know what teaching points to use to prompt the children within the lesson or to develop further in my next lesson plan (Table 7.11).

To reflect and extend on your planning in light of the details in this chapter consider continuing your ongoing assessment and observation development by observing colleagues and have colleagues come and observe you teach physical education and physical development sessions. If you are not able to watch each other within physical education perhaps you can try looking together at a movement that is occurring within the playground to help develop techniques. Here are some question prompts to aid you that you can try completing when watching each other or while watching movements:

1   What questions were asked during the warm-up session?

2   What body parts were referred to during the lesson activities?

3   Was any body part not referred to?

4   If a new skill was introduced were the preparation, action and recovery phases referred to?

5   Can you identify the next steps in the activity being taught for head, body, arms/hands and feet/legs?

6   What praise is being used within the lesson? What is being observed that is then transforming into praise?

7   Can you use any of the movement analysis templates to record and assess the movements being used?

8   What questions do the children ask each other?

9   What language/vocabulary are the children using to describe their movements, do they refer to body parts?

10   What targets/next steps or positive challenges are being identified?

Summary

This chapter has outlined the importance of observations and also how observations can inform assessments. It has considered numerous different templates and provided actual lesson examples of how to use and analyse movement and skills with the help of templates. It has highlighted the importance of objective, measurable assessment that can help to enhance the progress and development of the children's learning. The chapter has also aired caution as to the language that could potentially be used within a lesson and the impact this may have on children. It has also offered support prompts to help when starting to observe and assess within lessons and physical activity settings such as the break time.

Recommended reading

The following three texts are provided as follow-on reading:

1 Doherty, J. and Brennan, P. (2007). *Physical Education and Development 3–11 a Guide for Teachers*. Abingdon, Oxen: Routledge, Taylor and Francis Group.

2 Department for Education (DfE) (2013). *The National Curriculum in England. Key Stages 1 and 2 Framework Document.* London Crown.

3 Howells, K. (2015). 'Physical Education Planning'. In K. Sewell (ed.), *Planning the Primary National Curriculum: A Complete Guide for Trainees and Teachers.* Sage: London, pp. 262–76.

Chapter 8
Practical Issues in Physical Education

Chapter objectives

- Factors to consider when planning physical education
- Grouping children for physical education, including those who are gifted and talented
- Planning for risk and challenge within physical education
- How planning varies according to different learning environments within physical education
- Planning for physical education if there is a lack of equipment
- How staff can be employed effectively within primary physical education lessons

Introduction

A report by the All-Party Parliamentary Group (APPG) on a fit and healthy childhood physical education (2016) states, 'By imprinting a love of physical activity early into young people, we supply them with a roadmap for a healthy life, a way of managing stress, a base level for any physical challenge and a route into sports and other activities that can be lifelong' (p. 42).

This chapter will address how you can steer children along this 'roadmap' where they experience a range of learning environments to enable them to develop physically, socially, cognitively and emotionally, to help them realize their full potential as they start on their 'learning journey' from childhood to adulthood.

The chapter will enable you to be more confident in understanding the key practical considerations when planning for primary physical education. It is acknowledged that confidence and subject knowledge in physical education may vary widely and you have your own preferred teaching styles, which develops through time, experience and is reflective of your personality. The chapter will support you and other practitioners in your delivery of a quality physical education programme where all children's strengths are celebrated and areas for improvement targeted. It is hoped that this chapter will support continued professional development and will show how you can be more confident in your own planning and how this will positively impact on the learning journey taken by each child.

Pause for thought – *Thinking about planning*

What are the key considerations when planning for a physical education lesson?

Make a list of things that you feel are important when starting out on planning physical education. Beside each item on your list state why you are considering that item; is it an area that helps support the learning or does it help you as a teacher.

You may find it helpful to reflect on how you plan for other subjects such as numeracy and literacy, how the key considerations for planning these subjects also relate to physical education planning.

This chapter will draw upon previous chapters to build a picture of practical considerations and for addressing the physical literacy needs for all children for lifelong learning. The practical considerations will continue to explore physical education as an area that is crucial to the holistic development of all children regardless of their practical competence. It develops children in all the domains (Kirk 1993; Laker 2000; Howells 2015) and supports Whitehead's (2010) concept of physical literacy (see in Chapter 1). Physical education is so much more than 'just playing' or 'doing'. The full potential of physical education is as a valued learning experience where the individual child develops holistically and the teacher sets challenges to empower the learner to be responsible for their personal learning through a range of domains.

Following numerous research, for example, Metzler (2011) and Bunker and Thorpe (1982), regarding the value of using a range of pedagogical models to extend children's learning over the past years (including cooperative learning, teaching games for understanding, sport education and cross-curricular models, as discussed in Chapter 3), there appears to be still an over reliance or 'default setting' within primary physical education on the command or didactic style of teaching. Physical education fit for the twenty-first century should not consist of an isolated 'skill drill' approach which is ineffective in developing the needs of all learners (APPG 2016). A range of pedagogical models should be used through different practical activities therefore, equipping the young people to address their physical, mental and health needs as they move through different life stages. It should not be a one-model-fits-all approach; professional and personal reflection on the role of the teacher and their influence on the learning needs of individual children should be monitored and adapted accordingly. The practical considerations within this chapter are a reflection of this ideology and an opportunity for you to be reflective of your own practice.

Pause for thought – *Thinking about how you teach*

Reflecting on yourself, how do you teach physical education in the physical development sessions?

What is your preferred teaching style?

What do your physical education lessons 'look like'? Is the structure each week similar – do you use the same lesson by lesson approach? Do you vary the pedagogical approach to include all learning styles of the children?

Does the structure of your lessons vary according to the practical activity being taught?

The factors to consider when planning physical education

There are a number of factors that should be addressed when planning to teach physical education. Table 8.1 sets these considerations out as questions for you, and the table aims to guide you to answer the questions. It also includes inputs by key authors who have been previously referred to throughout the book to enable you to see how the readings and ideas can be applied to practical considerations. Effective planning should allow you to plan and deliver challenging, active and creative physical education lessons that motivate and enthuse children to achieve through a range of practical activities. The process should focus on the learning outcomes rather than the activity. For example: 'In PE on Tuesday we will be learning in dance to develop the use of different levels, (low, middle and high levels) to create simple patterns and then link them together to form a motif of movement on the floor and in the air', as opposed to 'in Physical Education on Tuesday we will be doing dance.'

This difference within the two examples illustrates a more children-centred approach, where active learning for a purpose is at the heart of the physical education lesson. The children will be able to understand *how* and *why* their learning is being developed, as well as developing movement vocabulary. It is a 'constructed' experience enabling children to build on previous knowledge and build meaning and relevance to new knowledge through an authentic experience of partnership between you and the children.

Pause for thought – *Thinking back*

Refer back to your own 'Key Consideration' list for planning in physical education.

Do your notes reflect Table 8.1?

What can you now do with this information to enhance your lessons plans in physical education?

Table 8.1 Questions to consider when practically planning physical education

Who are you teaching?	<ul><li>Age group</li><li>Previous experience</li><li>Any evidence of previous formative/summative assessment</li><li>Specific needs of the group, for example, inclusion issues, behaviour management considerations</li></ul>
What are you teaching?	<ul><li>National Curriculum requirements (DfE, 2013)</li><li>Practical concepts, for example, sending and receiving, locomotion, spatial awareness, body alignment in swimming</li><li>Social concepts, for example, team work in games; clear communication for problem-solving in outdoor and adventurous activities</li><li>Cognitive concepts, for example, understanding why you stand side on when sending; why we need to keep a tucked shape when completing a forward roll; the importance of physical activity to lead a healthy life</li><li>Through which practical activities will these concepts be addressed ensuring a broad practical curriculum, for example, invasion games, fundamental movement skills, dance, swimming, outdoor and adventurous activities</li><li>Physical education is not just 'playing' or 'doing' but learning to develop physical literacy (Whitehead 2010)</li><li>Health and fitness aspects to enable children to lead active, healthy lives</li></ul>
What are the learning outcomes?	<ul><li>What are the learning outcomes for the scheme of work?</li><li>What are the learning outcomes for the individual lesson?</li><li>What is the progression from the previous lesson and how will they continue to develop?</li><li>How do you keep the children active for sustained periods of time and also ensure learning is taking place? This is particularly important for addressing the recent concerns over the rising level of child obesity (APPG 2016)</li><li>Align learning outcomes to the content of the lesson (Biggs and Tang, 2007)</li><li>Share the learning outcomes at the beginning and end of the lesson to enable children to take an active role in their learning</li></ul>
What teaching styles will you use? What pedagogical approach/teaching strategy will be adopted?	<ul><li>What pedagogical approach will be used, for example, teaching games for understanding; sport education; technical model; cooperative learning, cross-curricular learning? (See also Chapter 3.)</li><li>Which teaching style/s from Mosston and Ashworth (1994) spectrum will be used to support the effective delivery of the chosen pedagogical approach?</li><li>Who will lead within the learning/teaching relationship; will it be characterized by teacher-led – didactic – command style – passive learning or child centred – guided discovery – divergent style – active learning?</li><li>How is the learning scaffolded?</li><li>What aspects of creativity will be utilized, for example, creative teaching and/or teaching for creativity? (Lavin 2008)</li><li>What are the children's preferred learning styles to ensure that the range of teaching approaches and styles have a constructive influence on learning?</li><li>What type of guidance will you use, for example, visual, verbal, manual?</li><li>Will any technology be used to enhance the learning and teaching relationship?</li></ul>

What learning environment are you using?	• Playground, hall, field, swimming pool, dance studio, multi-gym, local park/fields, outdoor pursuit centre, outdoor classroom • What equipment do you have to use – quality and quantity – and is it age-appropriate for physical development? • Timing of the lesson – actual length of teaching time (in addition to changing time); time of the day • Transitions from the classroom to the practical space
How will all learners be included?	• Differentiation of activities, for example, STTEP model (Chapter 3) • Grouping: ability, mixed, random, friendship; inclusion spectrum (Pickup et al. 2008) • Appropriate challenges and level of risk to meet their physical, social, cognitive and emotional development • There should be consideration for all children, including gifted and talented children • How do you include non-performers in the lesson to ensure that learning is still taking place even if they are not performing, for example, roles they can be involved in
How will you know learning has taken place?	• Align learning outcomes to the content of the lesson • What feedback will you provide to progress learning, for example, visual, verbal, manual • Observation of the physical activities • Questioning (Anderson et al. 2014) using a range of open and closed questions to encourage higher order thinking from Bloom's taxonomy from remembering, understanding through to applying, analysing, evaluating and creating • Self-assessment • Peer assessment • Record of learning that has occurred through detailed evaluation of the lesson which feeds forward to the planning for the next lesson • Use of other adults, for example, teaching assistant (TA), sports coach • Use of movement concepts, for example, Laban's (1975) body, space, dynamics and relationships to reflect on learning outcomes • Video evidence can be used by the teacher and/or the children • Alternative evidence through cross-curricular learning subjects, for example, children plot their run distances into graph during computing lessons; in English children create a game and write their rules showing accuracy and coherence of language and context or children 'interview' a sports man/woman showing competence in speaking and listening; linking geography and physical education, children can demonstrate their understanding of maps through an orienteering course
How can you ensure the environment is safe but children feel challenged?	• Subject knowledge of the teacher with clear and detailed planning • Professional development needs of individual staff for the different practical activities • School policy documents on Health and Safety/Child Welfare/Safeguarding • Risk assessments for each practical activity • Teacher position during the lesson to 'scan' the class for on-task, safe learning • Progressive, differentiated activities allowing appropriate challenges to be set according to child's developmental needs • Enabling children to take risks and be responsible for their decision making • Children should progress from working individually to working with partners to working in groups; consider how the activities develop from familiar to unfamiliar and directed to open • Regular equipment checks • Clothing of children and staff and other aspects such as jewellery • Environment factors, for example, clean, dry floor in the hall after lunch time; wet grass on the field • Behaviour management ensuring high-quality physical education taught in a safe environment

Grouping children for physical education including those who are gifted and talented

One practical issue for you may be 'how do I group children' with the focus being on the practical implications of the organization of this task rather than the intended learning outcomes for the lesson (see Table 8.1). What you want the children to learn and how this will be achieved is central to the answer to the question 'how do I group my children' (see Table 8.2). For example, if the outcome of the lesson is to move confidently in a range of ways (EYFS) or to engage in cooperative activities (KS1) (Figure 8.1) or to enjoy collaborating with each other (KS2) (Figure 8.2) then friendship grouping may be deemed appropriate. If the lesson outcome involves developing competence to excel and that the children are physically active for sustained periods of time then ability groupings would be relevant; if the lesson is in the swimming pool then ability grouping would be essential to enable you to differentiate by space/depth of the water for a safe environment.

One issue when considering grouping is to ensure that you vary the types of groupings you use for physical education so that the children do not work with the same group all the time. This will enable children's practical and personal (social) skills to be developed through a range of different experiences, thereby reinforcing the 'physical literacy' of each individual. However, for some lessons where the outcome is to develop linking movements into a sequence, for example, in gymnastics or into a

Figure 8.1 Key Stage 1 children in cooperative activities

Table 8.2 Other ways to group within physical education lessons

Friendship	• when you are new to the group and are not aware of their abilities
	• for when you want the children to feel confident, safe and secure in the learning environment, for example, introducing a new skill in throwing events in athletics; for developing trust in partner work in OAA
	• for when the learning environment is challenging, for example, apparatus work in gymnastics
	• to develop children's confidence, for example, developing a dance motif
Ability	• to include all learners at a level specific to their stage of skill learning, for example, some children developing hand–eye coordination for striking using a racket; one group working on collaborating with a partner to maintain a rally and one group applying skills playing against an opponent in a competitive scenario
	• when developing decision making and tactical awareness and complex game play
	• for safety, for example, ability groups in the swimming pool for differentiation by depth; when using hurdles in athletics; rock climbing on an outdoor trip
	• to consider changing ability groups throughout the year, for example, a child might be in the high-ability group for practical performance in dance but low-ability group for games-based activities
Mixed ability	• for developing a range of creative ideas in activities such as gymnastics and dance
	• for encouraging social integration and understanding of individual strengths
	• to create an 'even playing field', for example, relay's in athletics or swimming
Random	• when the 'make-up' of the group makes no difference to the activity
	• for problem-solving tasks
	• to develop creative minds
	• developing social cohesion
Non-performers	• how do you include all children in the class to ensure that active learning is taking place even if they are not performing?
	• for example, roles of referee, coach, scorer in sport education model
	• for example, working with a performer to act as their 'coach' providing positive feedback and personal support
	• for example, completing a 'learning support sheet' highlighting key teaching points from the lesson
	• for example, supporting the teacher by identifying good practice by the children and sharing this with the teacher explaining their reasons of choice

Figure 8.2 Key Stage 2 children collaborating

motif in dance, maintaining consistency with the same group week by week would be beneficial. Careful consideration of numbers at the start of the lesson is also important to avoid a child feeling 'left out' or isolated. You know your children best! You know from working with them in the classroom the dynamics of the relationships that they have; however, a note of caution: do not assume that this will be replicated in the practical space where some children may shine and others prefer to 'melt' into the background. Grouping children in different ways is a part of an effective differentiation strategy, which enables an inclusive curriculum promoting effective teaching to positively impact on learning for all learners regardless of their practical ability.

As well as considering the question of how to group the children you should also consider how the organization of grouping should occur to make all children feel valued. It would be good to think that we no longer witness the 'old fashioned elitist' view of having selected children at the front picking their teams. Think of the children 'left out' at the end of the selection process, emotionally having to cope with a peer saying

'Oh well! I suppose we have to have Alison then!' There is no place in physical education lessons for a child to feel worthless and unwanted; with the highly pressured environment of our present-day education system we should be doing all we can to build an individual's place of self and value in the school community.

Likewise, gender groupings have not been included in the above chart. In primary education physical education lessons tend to be non-gender-specific (unlike secondary education where physical education is often divided by gender) and, as such, divisions by gender may prove to be divisive and confrontational; although it may be that when children divide themselves into friendship groups then a gender divide naturally occurs. Recent research, Changing the Game for Girls: In Action (Women in Sport 2016) and Getting Girls Active campaigns by the Youth Sports

Trust (2014), highlights some of the barriers that girls may encounter in their physical education learning journey, especially the transition from primary to secondary schools. As such, you need to be sensitive to gender groupings and seek to inspire, motivate and enthuse all learners to perform in a safe, supportive environment where all children's voices are heard and valued.

Pause for thought – *Thinking about how to use questions to challenge children*

How do you use questioning to challenge the more able performers within your class?

Within other subjects, make a list the types of questions that you use and how you respond to your more able children's answers.

Now, can you apply this for physical education? Consider Bloom's Taxonomy and draw up some questions that you could ask targeting children's individual abilities.

Enablement of all learners to reach their full potential in a broad range of activities and across the learning domains should be reflected in the learning outcomes of individual lessons, and the grouping of children, including those children who are gifted and talented, should reflect this. However, there is a question to consider regarding the role of physical education in primary schools to 'create' the sports stars of tomorrow, building on London 2012 Games 'inspire a generation' (Coe 2011) and from the Rio Games in 2016. In support of Tinning (2011), who advocated that sport is merely one medium for the development of the physically educated child, schools need to be made aware that sport should not be the central focus of physical education. Primary physical education is unique in building the foundations for all learners to develop their physical literacy and movement skills to enable them to respond to the changing demands of the physical landscape that they will encounter on their learning journey from childhood to adult life. Some primary school children will progress to become the sporting stars of the future and teachers should seek to enthuse and motivate children to strive to reach their dreams and to maximize their potential. However, primary physical education aims to develop the children across generic skills that can be specialized and transferred into different sports, as the children move through secondary schooling. For example, a child may prove competent at sending and receiving using hands, feet and an implement and then refine these skills and apply them to the specialized activities of netball, football and hockey later on. Take the example of the Olympic, world and European skeleton champion Lizzy Yarnold, who was a 'keen athlete as a child … and tried her hand at most sports' (Yarnold 2014). In Lizzy's primary years, her teachers did not identify her as a future skeleton Olympic champion, but no doubt they instilled a love of physical activity, developing a range of skills across a variety of activities while fostering personal attributes such as determination, resilience, sportsmanship, responsibility, motivation to success. This should be central to all children as part of their physical education curriculum and it is from these strong foundations that the potential is seen, fostered and enhanced. When you consider a child to be talented, you can encourage this child to attend extracurricular clubs at the school, and, with the support of parents and carers, contact local clubs in the community for the child to attend. Local community clubs will also know if their local leisure trusts run 'Talent Athlete' (or similar) programmes. The key is that when planning, you should also seek to differentiate and challenge the talented children to achieve their maximum potential – as you would do for all your children regardless of their ability level.

Figure 8.3 demonstrates how Baileys' (2007) model of differentiation can be adapted to refer specifically to how the teacher can challenge the gifted and talented child in physical education. Likewise, with considerations given to presentation,

Figure 8.3 Bailey's (2007) model of differentiation used to support planning for gifted and talented children

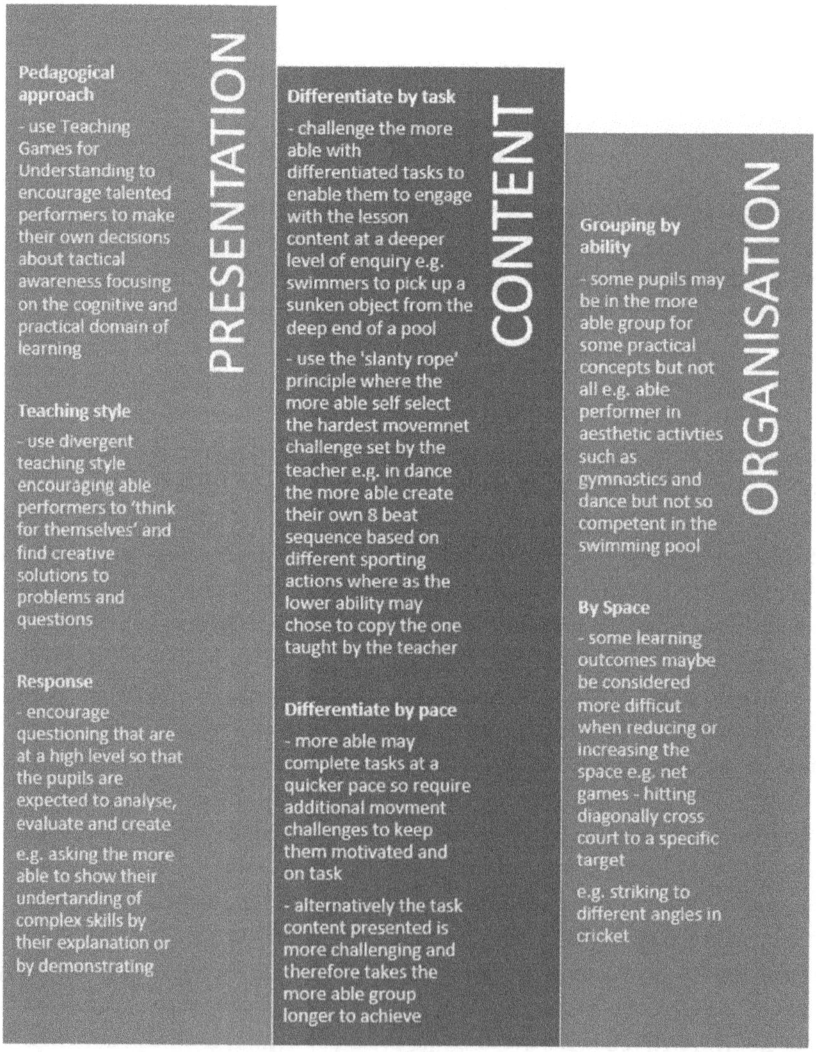

PRESENTATION

Pedagogical approach

- use Teaching Games for Understanding to encourage talented performers to make their own decisions about tactical awareness focusing on the cognitive and practical domain of learning

Teaching style

- use divergent teaching style encouraging able performers to 'think for themselves' and find creative solutions to problems and questions

Response

- encourage questioning that are at a high level so that the pupils are expected to analyse, evaluate and create

e.g. asking the more able to show their underanding of complex skills by their explanation or by demonstrating

CONTENT

Differentiate by task

- challenge the more able with differentiated tasks to enable them to engage with the lesson content at a deeper level of enquiry e.g. swimmers to pick up a sunken object from the deep end of a pool

- use the 'slanty rope' principle where the more able self select the hardest movemnet challenge set by the teacher e.g. in dance the more able create their own 8 beat sequence based on different sporting actions where as the lower ability may chose to copy the one taught by the teacher

Differentiate by pace

- more able may complete tasks at a quicker pace so require additional movment challenges to keep them motivated and on task

- alternatively the task content presented is more challenging and therefore takes the more able group longer to achieve

ORGANISATION

Grouping by ability

- some pupils may be in the more able group for some practical concepts but not all e.g. able performer in aesthetic activties such as gymnastics and dance but not so competent in the swimming pool

By Space

- some learning outcomes maybe be considered more difficut when reducing or increasing the space e.g. net games - hitting diagonally cross court to a specific target

e.g. striking to different angles in cricket

content and organization, this model can be utilized for any ability group in primary physical education.

> ## Pause for thought – *Thinking about organizing groups*
>
> How do you organize the children into groups?
>
> After reading the section above, are there any new ways in which you will now try to organize your groups for your next lesson?

How to plan for risk and challenge within physical education

What is risk and what is challenge within physical education? The triangle model of risk management in physical education adopted by the Association of Physical Education (AfPE) (Figure 8.4) suggests three areas that needed to be considered when exploring risk and challenge.

- People – including both children and the teacher (and other staff if being deployed within physical education)
- Context – including the learning environment being used, the equipment, the routines for the activity and transport, for example, off-site activity
- Organization – including how the class is grouped and how the learning environment is set up, the teaching styles used, how learning is prepared and progressed and any emergency action if an accident or incident takes place

Children want to, and need to, take risks and the teacher and school policies should aim to 'respond to these needs and wishes by offering children stimulating, challenging environments for exploring and developing their abilities' (Ball et al. 2012). In doing this, the level of risk can be managed so that children are challenged

Figure 8.4 Triangle model of risk management

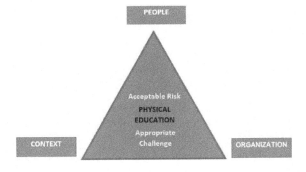

but not put at risk of injury or harm. The mantra of 'good practice is safe practice' (Whitlam 2005) is a sensible one reinforcing the importance of careful planning and defining 'good risks' as those that engage and challenge children and support their growth, learning and development. However, it should be highlighted that taking risks in physical education does not need to be associated with activities that are 'dangerous'. For example, when children take risks in decision making for game play: a child may choose to send a long pass, in order to gain a shooting position closer to the target. A long pass poses a 'risk' as it gives the defenders more time and space to intercept the ball, but if the risk 'pays off', then your team is in a stronger position to be successful with the goal-shooting opportunity. Reflection on risks taken in game play can then be evaluated, by the children and supported by you, to enhance the children's understanding of the application of the skill and the effect of the risks taken as part of their decision making.

Considerations for the effective planning and delivery of practical activities should include 'risk–benefit' analysis (Hodgson and Bailie 2011), whereby the benefits significantly outweigh the risks and the 'balance' has been carefully scrutinized. With regard to the three components of the risk management model (Figure 8.4), some steps will be discussed in this chapter to support you in balancing this risk, such as grouping, teaching approaches, lesson routines and different learning environments. You must consider what further steps you can take to ensure that the children are challenged and that the scales are tipped heavily in favour of the 'benefit' side, as Whitlam (2005) proposes that achieving a balanced risk–benefit decision involves the application of a series of good teaching and good organization principles.

One important aspect of managing risk, but not creating a 'sterile' environment for the children's learning in physical education, is aligning the progression of learning outcomes and differentiated activities to the skill abilities and potential of the children. Therefore, you need to revise and build on previous learning experiences to enable the children to make informed decisions about what is the 'right' thing to do. For example, if you plan to use the 'movement tables' for exploring the fundamental movement skill of jumping from a high level onto a mat, what movement principles should you have taught previously? The children cannot be expected to jump from a height with confidence, competence and consideration for personal safety, and the safety of those around them, if the principles of body management and control on landing when jumping on the floor have not been understood and experienced first by the children. Differentiation and progressive skill learning (referred to in Chapter 6) are crucial aspects of teachers' planning and children's learning that will balance the 'risk–benefit' analysis. While it is 'good' that you are worried about children hurting themselves in physical education (as this shows you care), this fear should not prevent you from planning exciting opportunities for learning to occur across the domains: physically, socially, cognitively and emotionally.

Reinforcing expected standards of behaviour and following routines are important for you to manage the risks associated with any activity and for the children to know *what* they should do, and *why*, considering the consequences of their actions; for example, children staying behind the 'safety line' when throwing an object for throwing events in athletics or holding onto the side of the pool when the teacher is giving out the next set of instructions. Organizational routines are also an integral part of a well-planned lesson promoting high-quality learning and teaching. For example, ensuring all children warm up and cool down; handing out of equipment safely and making sure that no loose balls are left in the playing area to prevent accidents. Following guidelines set by you will also be an important aspect of the children's learning about the need to minimize risk; for example, if you explain that you do not want the hockey stick lifted above shoulder height due to the risk of injury to other children in the set space, then this 'rule' must be adhered to. After setting out equipment such as the wall bars in gymnastics, the children should know that they must not go onto these until you have checked that the equipment is secure and safe.

Pause for thought – *Thinking about off-site visit and safety within lessons*

Read your school's policies (or that of a school known to you) and your physical education and physical activity policies on safe practice and guidance for off-site activities.

Consider the key safety considerations from this document and how they can be implemented into your planning for primary physical education lessons.

How planning varies according to different learning environments within physical education

There are key principles of planning for physical education that will be replicated in all environments used for physical education. Such key elements have been addressed in the beginning of this chapter and some will be highlighted further here to address unique features of specific environments. To ensure that learning will take place and that the children are partners in the process, the learning outcomes should be clearly explained by you. Redelius et al. (2015) concluded that 'if goals are well articulated by teachers, the students are most likely to both understand and be aware of the learning outcomes' (p. 2) and that if the objectives are not explained the children will not know what they are supposed to do and their learning experiences will be less valued and meaningful.

Management of the environment in physical education is a key component to ensure a safe working environment for all (Shaughnessy 2008) and this should be a further consideration when planning for different environments. You should refer to the latest edition of Safe Practice in Physical Education, School Sport and Physical Activity, which has been written by the AfPE (2016) to ensure that your own working practices are aligned to the recommendations by the AfPE (see also

Chapter 6). Your own physical education coordinator and head teacher will be familiar with this document; it offers advice for the safe practice of all of the practical activity areas in physical education curriculum, and helps to support your own school policies on health and safe practice, as well as your physical education and physical activity policies.

High expectations of the children should be a prerequisite for effective planning in any physical education environment. You should be prepared to adapt your plans accordingly to the needs of the children as the lesson develops. Being a role model is an important aspect of motivating children to participate in physical activity and, as such, you should be dressed appropriately to enable you to teach effectively. If we are expecting the children to wear their kit to enable them to learn effectively, and safely, then you should replicate this in your choice of clothing (as highlighted in Chapter 3). Teaching, for example, the sideways stance for sending skills will be ineffective as a visual demonstration if children cannot see an accurate picture. The school management team should support staff in their ability to come dressed in appropriate clothing if they are teaching physical education that particular day or they should provide time for the teacher to get changed. We would not expect to teach other subjects without the correct equipment, so why should we settle for anything less in physical education?

A routine is important in any environment for primary physical education for both you and the children for the 'smooth' organization of the lesson. However, to develop responsible and reactive learners a routine that is too restricted may impact negatively on the intended learning outcomes in a constructive, problem-based learning model; therefore, you need to consider the lesson from a range of different perspectives to ensure that the children's learning is the main priority. The physical education lesson begins from when the children start to get changed and not just from when they enter the specific learning environment. Getting changed for a purpose will help with the speediness of changing which is often cited anecdotally as a barrier to time management in primary physical education. An example of good practice is to share the highlights of the intended outcomes of the lesson with the children before they get changed, so they are motivated to get ready quickly to start learning. Once changed, the children, rather than just sitting on the floor waiting for the others, should be encouraged to engage with active learning opportunities, enabling you to make use of all the available time for children to learn within physical education. Examples of active learning across a broad range of skills and activities could include:

- Discussing the learning outcomes written on the board with a partner
- Watching and analysing video evidence of learning from the previous week
- Looking at the gymnastics apparatus cards and beginning to plan their response to the movement challenge
- Getting into their 'groups' and discussing the tactics from the previous games lesson and how they might adapt them this week to make them more successful
- Listening to the piece of music to be used in the dance lesson to help support responses to timing and rhythm

- Considering how to pace themselves for the athletics lesson based on keeping active for a sustained period of time
- Consulting the school map and planning their route around the orienteering course

Movement from the classroom into the practical space should be orderly and transfer of equipment should be considered to enable learning to take place as soon as the children arrive at the venue for the lesson. Once at the venue, active learning should start as soon as possible after any relevant safety information is given and the learning outcomes shared with specific reference to key learning opportunities for the children. The lesson should include a warm-up session and progressive movement challenges differentiated to the children's needs to allow for learning to take place across the domains. Constructive feedback should enable the children to make progress and understand how they can develop and apply their skills across the range of activities. High standards or behaviour should be expected and reinforced. A cool-down activity should be planned and the learning outcomes should be addressed again to assess the level of the children's knowledge and understanding which may transpire through observation and or questioning. Equipment should be returned and the venue should be left in an orderly fashion for the next user. Returning to the classroom and getting changed should also be considered a part of the lesson and consideration should be given to any extrinsic motivational 'awards' such as 'Physical Education Performer of the Day' or 'Most Supportive Physical Education Pupil'. These motivational awards can vary given the type of lesson being taught and the intended learning outcomes. Figure 8.5 illustrates that 'fair play' was a focus

Figure 8.5 Fair play award

of the social skills being developed within a physical education lesson based on the Sport Education Model.

Teacher position is another important aspect for planning in any environments for physical education. When addressing the whole class, you should be in a position where all children can see the demonstration (and hear the verbal commands), preferably with the demonstration being shown from a variety of angles to give an accurate picture. When providing feedback to an individual or small group, you should be in a position 'open' to the rest of the class so that you can scan the space to ensure all children are safe and on task. During the lesson, consider where you are positioning yourself and ensure that you are able to move around all the activities taking place, so you can either observe your focus group or observe the whole class. In Figure 8.6, the teacher is positioned on the outside of all the activities (a circle has been used to mark her position); she is observing all the children and in particular those in front of her who are jumping in and out of large hoops. (See Figure 8.6, and Chapter 7 for more on observations.)

If your school is taking your children off-site for activities, for example, swimming at the local leisure centre or the Year 6 residential trip to an outdoor activities centre, then you must consult the school and county policies to verify that their planning covers all aspects of health, safety and child welfare and safe guarding. Ask for advice and help from members of your senior management team and experienced staff within your school/setting especially if it is your first time taking children off-site. Another key element for planning in different environments is that of space, space that allows not only to move and learn safely but also to achieve the learning outcomes and to introduce differentiated movement challenges to include all learners.

Figure 8.6 Teacher positioning

For example, if the learning outcome is to develop creating width in attack for games play then the space to allow for width to be created, must be given to the children to allow them to achieve this. If the learning outcome is to apply accurate stride patterns between hurdles in athletics, then the choice of hurdles should be differentiated by the height and distance between them; and children should be empowered to make these decisions knowing their own abilities. If early years' children are discovering the most effective technique to send an object to a target, then they should have the space to move the target towards or away from them allowing for learning in line with their motor development.

It is important that for every learning environment the children know the expected standards of behaviours and for you to share with the children your command for 'stop, look at me and listen'. This is important not only if you need to gain the children's attention immediately due to a concern for their safety (for example, in the swimming pool or when using gymnastics apparatus), but also to enable feedback or further instructions to be given to support the next stage of learning. Planning for transitions between learning activities is another consideration. In any environment in primary physical education, there are changes that may involve groupings, equipment, space, time for feedback and questioning. These should be carefully considered so that the management of these transitions does not disrupt the flow of the lesson leading to children being off task and potentially increasing the chance of standards of behaviour falling below expectations. For example, if the children are going to get into groups once outside (and it is cold and wet!) then why not organize them into groups as soon as they are changed in the classroom, where you have set boundaries and the environmental conditions are 'on your side'. If the children are going to have a ball each and then the next activity they have one ball between four you need to consider how will you organize this to make sure that any equipment not being used, is safely away from the learning space. In swimming how will you organize the handing out of floats for one activity and then collecting them back in?

Each area in which you teach physical education is unique, and is specific to your individual school setting. Even if a physical education environment is not available for teaching on a specific day, for example, the outdoor ground conditions are dangerous from being too muddy and wet and the hall is being used for other activities, do not 'cancel' physical education. The classroom could be used, for some simple problem-solving skills, some video analysis of key movement skills, or to conduct a physical education 'quiz' to reinforce the value of the subject to the children. Presented below are considerations for planning in different physical education environments, including indoor halls, playground or outdoor spaces, school field, off-site fields, swimming pools and outdoor and adventure centres (if you do not have your own specific area within your educational setting). Each area is considered and some questions and thoughts are posed that you need to reflect upon as the teacher/practitioner before you start planning your lesson:

Indoor hall

1 Check if floor is clean, dry and non-slippery

2 Ensure any equipment/furniture is moved to the side or removed, for example, piano, lunch tables, assembly chairs. If they remain in the teaching space set off the area to be used with cones or flat, non-slip markers

3 All equipment, for example, gymnastics and games equipment, should be regularly checked and any broken or damaged equipment should not be used

4 Any fixed apparatus, for example, wall bars should be checked for accurate fixing before being used (Figure 8.7). The gymnastics wall bars have locks at the bottom of each section that drop a bolt into the floor, it is important to turn these so that the top of the handle is at 90 degrees, so that they do not go loose. The ladders that are attached both have a locking bolt at the bottom with hooks to secure them to the different heights on the main apparatus.

5 Ensure that all electrical equipment, for example, music equipment has been tested for safe use

6 Determine how you want to indicate to the children, where you want them to land or rotate (Figure 8.8). With gymnastics there are two reasons to use mats, one is for comfort, for example, for rotational movements along the floor, and one is for landing on. If you 'mat out' the whole floor, the children

Figure 8.7 Gymnastics wall apparatus

Figure 8.8 Placement of mats by the wall apparatus for jumping and landing

will be confused as to what you want them to do. In Figure 8.8, the mat is being used to encourage the children to jump from part of the wall apparatus and to land. This is the only part of the apparatus where a mat is placed next to the equipment so this is the only part that you are expecting the children to jump.

Playground/outdoor space (depends on the season and weather conditions)

1 Check playground for leaves, moss that may be a slip hazard. Can these be removed prior to any PE lesson to avoid having to 'cancel' physical education?

2 Check that no rubbish has been left, for example, plastic/glass water bottles

3 Are there any painted lines to create a boundary or do you need to create one with flat, non-slip markers?

4 Where is the equipment stored and how will you move it to where you are teaching?

5 Where will the equipment be during the lesson to avoid any loose equipment, for example, balls being a hazard to the teacher and children?

6 If striking/hitting an object are there are windows in the buildings – which direction will you tell the children to hit/strike?

7 Check that any fixed equipment, for example, football/netball goals, is secure

8 Due to the environment and space available for the children to move, a whistle will be useful as a command to 'stop, look and listen'

9 Will you be teaching alone or with support, for example, with the help of a teaching assistant; this may become important to consider if a child gets injured or needs to leave the outdoor learning space and be out of your sight

10 Sketch out your plans for the area before setting it out, so the children or another adult can be involved in helping to set out the area (Figure 8.9 shows the sketch and Figures 8.10 and 8.11 show the actual area). Is it possible to set out the outdoor space before the lesson to allow for more learning time during the lesson?

Figure 8.9 Sketch of activities layout

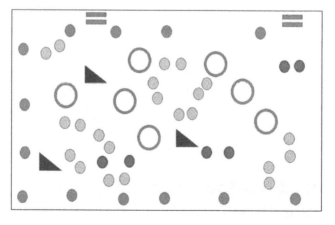

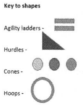

Figure 8.10 Outdoor space set up (matches previous sketch)

Figure 8.11 Opposite angle of outdoor space set up with equipment cupboard (right) and equipment for the activities (left)

School field

1 Check there is no rubbish left out in the teaching areas

2 Set out clearly marked boundaries

3 How will you transfer the equipment from the storage area to the teaching area?

4 What happens if a child has an injury/feels poorly or you need additional support – what line of communication do you have to connect to the school, for example, school mobile, walkie-talkie

5 Whistle for 'stop, look and listen'

6 Check for wet and slippery grass – depending on the activity being taught, for example, jumping would be considered dangerous but running for pace would be suitable

7 Is the large equipment wet and slippery? (Figure 8.12). How many children can be on one equipment at one time? Does your school have a directional route that needs to be taken? Refer to your school policies for guidance

8 If you have a long jump sand pit, is it clear of any rubbish or other hazards?

Figure 8.12 Large equipment used in outdoor and adventure activities

Off school site such as local park/field

1 School 'off-site medical/consent' forms
2 Organization of transporting children safely to and from the off-site teaching space
3 Ratio of staff to children
4 Medical supplies required for individual children needs
5 Safety of children if they go 'out of sight', for example, in an orienteering course
6 Transport of equipment to and from the site, or is there equipment stored at the venue for use?
7 What happens if a child has an injury/feels poorly or you need additional support – what line of communication do you have to connect to the school, for example, school mobile, walkie-talkie?
8 Consider active learning time, if time is taken out of the lesson for walking to and from the off-site location

Swimming pool/leisure centre

1 The centre should have their own pool safety operating procedures (PSOP)
2 School 'off-site medical/consent' forms
3 Pre-swimming instructions to parents/children regarding swimming kit and organization of the day
4 Transport arrangements to and from the pool
5 Required child/teacher ratio
6 Transfer of equipment or prior information on whether equipment will be available to use at the pool
7 Supervision of changing areas and pool side
8 Contact with the school for the teacher in charge
9 Medical supplies for individual children's needs
10 Pool first aid and staff training/qualifications
11 DBS checks for all staff
12 Qualified staff to teach swimming
13 Life guard provided by the pool (in addition to the swimming teachers)
14 Male and female staff supporting activities (if relevant)

Outdoor and adventurous activities centre

1   The centre should have their own health and safety policies

2   School 'off-site medical/consent' forms

3   Medical supplies for individual children's needs

4   Public liability insurance

5   Up-to-date qualifications of all the staff and DBS checks

6   Safeguarding policy

7   First aid provision and staff training

8   Staff/child ratio

9   Male and female staff supporting activities (if relevant)

Planning for physical education if there is a lack of equipment

Physical education storage cupboards are either like 'treasure chests' or dirty, dusty places with poorly organized equipment left lying around making finding what you need difficult! Equipment has usually been collected over a number of years through school funds, supermarket rewards schemes, donated by PTA, or bought using some of the sport premium funding (DfE 2016). Your school could collect additional equipment, by becoming involved in healthy living schemes. For example, the Jump Rope for Heart (JRFH), the British Heart Foundation's (BHF) skipping challenge, which provides participating schools with over £100 worth of free skipping ropes, or the BHF Ultimate Dodgeball Challenge with £30 worth free kit for children who help raise funds for life-saving research as well as for the school. Primary physical education equipment is usually stored in a cupboard in the school hall (Figure 8.13) or in a 'storage shed' situated on the playground/field; some schools may even have more than one storage facility for 'indoor' and 'outdoor' equipment. It is important that the physical education coordinator, and relevant staff, consider the most appropriate way to store equipment for ease of access at all times and for the cupboard to be kept tidy and well organized to avoid any potential damage to equipment or for the safety of staff and children. 'Large' gymnastics equipment is often stored in the school hall itself so the wider school community should know the appropriate use of this equipment, for example, movement tables should not be climbed and sat upon for assemblies or during lunchtimes.

Wherever the equipment is stored, the space *should* be well organized, clean and dry with clearly labelled storage bags and/or boxes. The equipment should enable the teachers to cover a broad range of practical activities and should be differentiated (for

Figure 8.13 'Typical' physical education cupboard

example, balls of different weights, size, colour and rackets/bats of varying surface area such as short tennis rackets, Kwick cricket bats, wooden bats) to allow for access by all children in line with their physical and cognitive development. Some schools may also have 'Inclusive Sports' equipment such as goalballs, blindfolds, New Age Kurling and Boccia. It should be possible for children to transport the equipment, to encourage responsible learners and to learn lifelong lifting and moving skills. Another consideration is whether the physical education equipment is available for use by the children before school, at breaks or lunchtimes or after school therefore developing a positive whole-school approach to physical literacy (although breakfast and after-school clubs often have their own equipment that they keep for their sole use). Does the school provide bike or scooter racks that are covered to support physical development through non-curriculum activities?

Not all schools will have plentiful and high-quality equipment. However, simple organization of equipment, for example, keeping your cones in colour-coded piles, will help with setting out particular areas within your learning environment, as well as helping with key vocabulary for early years. Some key equipment for early years to help with the development of spatial awareness and personal space is that of 'spots' (non-slip, flat markers). These are available in different colours and shapes/sizes and can be used, as 'home spots' whereby the children return to their own space and own spot. The spots can be used to map out on the floor patterns to help children develop a range of locomotor movement skills. They can be colour coded to support acquisition of key vocabulary as well as space development and also helping to build collaborate and cooperative learning situations, which are all important for early years' movement development.

The key to being able to cope with a potential lack of equipment, especially in games, is to *be creative*; for example, if you are looking at sending and receiving using hands you could use netballs, throw shuttlecocks, use tennis balls or balloons (check that children do not have latex allergies). The range of equipment and how this impacts on the skills being learnt can enhance children's psychomotor and cognitive domains of learning in physical education. You could also be creative and differentiate by group and equipment; for example, if the learning outcome is sending and receiving a ball, one group may have rugby balls to use, another group may have netballs and yet another group may be using sponge balls. The same idea of being creative could be applied to using different rackets; use tennis as well as badminton rackets with different types of balls and shuttlecocks. For striking and fielding, there should be no specific requirement to use a bat to strike the ball; hand/s and feet can also be used therefore developing hand and eye as well as foot and eye coordination prior to adding a stick or bat.

If the number of balls is less and every child does not have a ball, this does not have to be a limitation for providing a quality learning experience. A ball between two means that children can construct activities where they are both involved, or one child could be using a ball while the other offers feedback/scaffolds learning. For example, if one kicks a ball against a target while partner observes from the side and gives feedback, it keeps a tally chart on their level of accuracy. This kind of practice would then allow for links to numeracy and language, through the use of key vocabulary and technical language development. If you have the children in threes or fours (to apply the practice to cricket), this would allow you to use the reciprocal teaching style (Mosston and Ashworth 2002) when, for example, one child self-feeds to hit a stationary ball from a batting tee, hitting towards a target area. Another child observes using a criteria sheet to check the performance of the hitting technique and one/two children acts as fielders (short and long) and to collect loose balls and to feed the ball back to the batter to hit again. The children would then change roles after six hits (reflecting the numbers of balls in an 'over' for cricket.) Other areas to consider if there is a lack of equipment in games are the use of different pedagogical models (as discussed in Chapter 3) to help utilize players in a range of activities and to make game playing meaningful. By using the Sport Education Model or Teaching Games for Understanding model (see Chapter 3) children are engaged in constructing knowledge and understanding through game-based activities or by taking on different roles to ensure competent, literate and enthusiastic sports people. These models move away from the 'skills drills' of command style teaching and the requirement for a large amount of equipment for each child to use.

For gymnastics, if there are not enough mats for one each, children can share a mat between two. This helps to develop cooperative learning, trust and patience, allowing for variation in movement patterns and the development of unison (at the same time) and cannon (one after the other) pair work. Sharing a mat will also encourage the children to develop, apply and respond to Laban's (1975) movement categories of body, space, dynamics and relationships (as discussed in Chapter 6). Lack of equipment for gymnastics may also imply limited apparatus for applying floor work to different heights and challenges, the school hall having no fixed wall bars or limited space in the hall. Apparatus is often set up in a linear fashion due to a lack (or perceived lack) of space in the learning environment. If set up as such there is often an expectation by the teacher that children will start and finish at a predetermined point and that all children will start from the same place which will result in queues while children wait for 'their turn'. Unfortunately, children can also become passive learners as the teacher expects them to 'walk up the bench, step onto the box top, jump on to the mat, travel along the mat and hold a balance to finish'. To engage learners, you could refer to the learning outcomes of the lesson, for example, 'to use different ways of travelling using all the apparatus focussing on body control'. The children are then encouraged to explore the apparatus at the same time devising their personal responses to the movement challenge. Another solution could be to consider setting up a few 'apparatus stations' and then managing how the children move around these for equality of opportunity within the same lesson or moving the children on a week-by-week basis so they change between different stations over several lessons.

A lack of equipment, for example, floats or noodles, in swimming or in athletics, may be seen as a barrier to effective learning. As previously discussed, if you are creative with your organization of the learning space then this can be overcome. For example, in swimming, children can work in pairs with one of the children waiting for their turn holding onto the poolside. A child can be engaged in observation of the performer, providing constructive feedback on the intended learning outcomes for the activity when the swimmer returns to the side. For athletics, effective grouping of children can also allow time for children to be involved in a range of roles within the learning process, for example, one child jumping for distance, one child measuring, one child recording the jump and providing feedback.

Another consideration for a lack of equipment is to use playground equipment such as painted lines, squares (Figure 8.14) hopscotch markings as well as climbing frames during physical education lessons. This will help support the children to explore and develop gross and fine motor skills and enable the children to develop their confidence and competence to use this equipment safely. This can then be extended to child-initiated play outside of the physical education environment. The outdoors, and any playground musical equipment, can also be used to create sound and emotion to encourage young children to respond through movement in the natural outdoor environment. The outdoors should be viewed in terms of the Affordance Theory (Gibson 2015); while you might think that the climbing frame can be used as a climbing frame, to an early year's child the space underneath might

Figure 8.14 Playground markings

be the home of magical creatures or the top as a lookout to catch the pirates invading across the sea. The space 'affords' a range of different movement possibilities to the child – why should you dictate what they do with the space around them?

Pause for thought – *An activity to complete:*

Complete an audit of the equipment available in your school for physical education.

Does it provide opportunities for learning across all the age ranges and physical abilities?

Do you feel that the learning environment would be enhanced by purchasing more (or different types) of equipment? Discuss your thoughts with your physical education coordinator.

How staff can be effectively deployed within primary physical education lessons

Since the introduction of the sport premium funds (DfE 2016) a number of schools have employed the services of a coaching company to deliver curriculum (and extracurricular) physical education lessons, while the class teacher is released for their PPA time. The introduction of UK Government funds to increase the quality of physical education provision in primary schools was initially welcomed and an important step to increasing the value of physical education as an important subject in the education of all young children. However, using the funds to 'hire' coaching companies appears to have had a negative impact on the quality and experiences of other staff to teach physical education in some schools. The generation next executive summary (Randell et al. 2016) on initial teacher education for primary schooling showed that less student teachers are teaching physical education as 'the coaching company does all the Physical Education', rather than being, as hoped, a support mechanism to build CPD and confidence levels of teachers and trainees. This will affect the motivation, confidence and ability of inexperienced staff to teach a subject that many feel worried about due to its unique nature of learning through a range of environments. If a teacher is unable to teach physical education in their schools how will they develop and extend their knowledge and understanding? It would appear that the workforce is being 'deskilled' rather than being 'upskilled'.

Through using a supportive model the class teacher can teach their own class or for the teacher to work alongside the coaches to share knowledge of the children and the teaching/learning relationship while the coaches can support the teacher with developing specific subject knowledge (as highlighted in Chapter 3). Some coaches may be a qualified level 1 coach, for example in football, but how does that make them automatically able to teach gymnastics, dance and athletics? Do they know and understand the National Curriculum? What knowledge do they have of child development? How is their lesson evaluated or teaching monitored by the school? A proposal to designate a physical development/physical activity coordinator in every early years' setting and for all state primary schools to have a physical education specialist is a welcomed recommendation by the Next Generation Report (Randell et al. 2016). This supports the importance of early years and primary children in their acquisition of key elements for developing 'physical literacy'.

If you are supported by a teaching assistant in physical education lessons, this could be an ideal set up, as they will know and understand the class and can be an integral part of the teaching and learning process in physical education as much as they are in other subjects. Some teachers may also be supported by movement specialists for specific children such as a physiotherapist; this often happens in special education schools. It is also important for you to have a positive working relationship with the physical education coordinator so that they can support the planning, delivery and evaluation of the lessons and signpost you to any professional development opportunities to increase confidence and subject knowledge. Similarly, a physical education specialist from a secondary school setting, for example, from an 'all age academy', may also become involved to support the physical education coordinator and the teachers.

Some activities do require specific qualifications, swimming, for example. In the scenario of a class using a local swimming pool the school may employ two qualified swimming teachers to work alongside one member of staff from the school who also holds the appropriate certification. The class can then be divided into groups allowing for differentiated learning activities to challenge the children and minimize the risk of children being in an area of the pool that is not in line with their swimming ability. As well as swimming, many off-site activities are often taught by specialists in the different disciplines, for example, canoeing, rock climbing or archery. If all the necessary safety and safeguarding checks and risk assessments are completed by the school, in conjunction with the centre, then these activities will serve to bring an exciting and challenging dimension to the curriculum.

Your school could also utilize the local community and/or choose to invite activity specialists, for example, a handball coach, a yoga teacher, a dance teacher specializing in African dance. This should be a two-way process with the class teacher learning from the specialist and developing their own subject knowledge and confidence so that they can teach this activity again. There may be parents/grandparents with a specific interest or qualification that could support physical education teaching in the curriculum or for extracurricular time. Parents and grandparents could also introduce activities from different times and cultures to enrich the learning environment and potentially promote international perspectives (APPG 2016). These suggestions will also support the school to deliver a broad range of practical activities rather than the traditional focus on a games-based curriculum.

Pause for thought – *Thinking about deploying staff*

How are staff deployed within your setting for physical education?

Do you know why they are deployed in the way they are? Does it relate to subject knowledge and experience or for other operational reasons?

How can the school support your professional development in physical education to ensure that you are not being 'deskilled' if external agencies are teaching physical education lessons?

Summary

This chapter has outlined the importance of a range of learning and teaching principles emphasizing quality delivery as paramount with the focus on the learning needs of each child to reach their potential as physically literate individuals. As the APPG (2016) report declares: 'PE can be a key tool in the development of robust and determined young people whose confidence is rooted in the success of their accomplishments and who have formulated strategies to succeed in both physically and mentally challenging situations' (p. 42).

This declaration reinforces some key messages from the chapter; a child-centred teaching approach empowers children to construct their knowledge and understanding through clearly defined learning outcomes set by you guiding them to realize their potential through differentiated challenges across the range of domains.

Teaching physical education in the primary school is a rewarding role but one that requires commitment and hard work. It is hoped that this chapter will build your confidence in subject knowledge and application of some key considerations and initiate an enquiring mind to consider how your teaching impacts on the level of children's learning. The importance of physical activity in a range of environments and through a variety of activities has also, hopefully, confirmed the value of physical literacy for lifelong learning. As previously highlighted, physical education is more than just 'doing'; it should inspire, enthuse, excite and challenge every child through all their senses to enable them to be the very best they can be.

Recommended reading

The following three texts are provided as follow-on reading:

1 Bailey, R. (2007). Chapter 4: Lesson Organization and Management. *Teaching Physical Education. A Handbook for Primary and Secondary School Teachers.* London: Routledge, pp. 59–79.

2 Hodgson, C. and Bailie, M. (2011). Chapter 3: *Risk Management. Philosophy and Practice.* In M. Berry and C. Hodgson (eds), *Adventure Education. An Introduction*, pp. 46–62.

3 Zwozdiak-Myers, P. (2010). Chapter 5: Communication in PE. In S. Capel and M. Whitehead (eds), *Learning to Teach Physical Education in the Secondary School.* London and New York: Routledge, pp. 61–79.

Bibliography

All-Party Parliamentary Group (2016). A Fit and Health Childhood. *Physical Education.* London: All-Party Parliamentary Group.

Almond, L. (2016). International Physical Literacy Association. *The Primacy of Movement: Some implications for Physical Literacy.* Available at: https://www.physical-literacy.org.uk/primacy-of-movement/ (Accessed 2 August 2016).

Almond, L. and Afonso, A. (2014). *Objections to the use of Fundamental Movement Skills as central to Physical Literacy.* International Physical Literacy Association. Available at: https://www.physical-literacy.org.uk/objections-to-the-use-of-fundamental-movement-skills-as-central-to-physical-literacy/ (Accessed 2nd August 2016).

Almond, L. and Lambden, K. (2016). *Promoting Purposeful Physical Play in the Early Years through Physical Literacy. A Self-Learning Programme for Early Years Settings and their Practitioners.* Loughborough: Step into Purposeful Play.

Amateur Swimming Association (2010). National Curriculum Training Programme.

Anderson, L. W., Krathwohl, D. R., Airasian P. W., Cruikshank, K. A., Mayer, R. E., Pintrich, P. R., Raths, J., Wittrock, M. C. (2014). *A Taxonomy for Learning, Teaching, and Assessing: A revision of Bloom's.* Upper Saddle River: Pearson.

Armour, K. and Harris, J. (2013). Making the Case for Developing New PE-for-Health Pedagogies. *Quest,* 65 (2), 201–19.

Association for Physical Education (2008). A Manifesto for a World Class System of Physical Education. Available at http://www.afpe.org.uk/images/stories/Manifesto.pdf (Accessed 1 October 2016).

Association for Physical Education (2015). *Health Position Paper.* Available at: http://www.afpe.org.uk/physical-education/wp-content/uploads/afPE_Health_Position_Paper_Web_Version2015.pdf (Accessed 29 October 2016),

Association of Physical Education (AfPE) (2016). *Safe Practice in Physical Education, School Sport and Physical Activity.* Worcester: AfPE.

Bailey, R. (2007). *Teaching Physical Education. A Handbook for Primary and Secondary School Teachers.* London: Routledge.

Ball, D., Gill, T. and Spiegal, B. (2012). *Managing Risk in Play Provision: Implementation guide.* Play England on behalf of the Play Safety Forum by National Children's Bureau. Available at: http://www.playengland.org.uk/media/172644/managing-risk-in-play-provision.pdf (Accessed 18 November 2016).

Bee, H. (2000). *The Developing Child.* 9th edn. Boston: Allyn and Bacon.

Bernstein, E., Phillips, S. and Silverman, S. (2011). Attitudes and Perceptions of Middle School Students Towards Competitive Activities in Physical Education. *Journal of Teaching in Physical Education,* 30(1), 69–83.

Biggs, J. and Tang, C. (2007). *Teaching for Quality Learning at University,* 3rd edn. Buckingham: SRHE and Open University Press.

Blair, R. and Capel, S. (2008). Intended or Unintended? Issues Arising from the Implementation of the UK Government's 2003 Schools Workforce Remodelling Act. *Perspectives in Education,* 26 (2), 105–21.

Bruner, J. (1983). *Child's Talk: Learning to Use Language.* New York: Norton.

Bunker, D. and Thorpe, R. (1982). A Model for the Teaching of Games in Secondary Schools. *Bulletin of Physical Education*, 18 (1), Spring.

Bunker, D. and Thorpe, R. (1982). in Griffin, L. and Butler, J. (2005). *Teaching Games for Understanding: Theory, Research and Practice.* Champaign: Human Kinetics.

Burton, D. and Raedeke, T. D. (2008). *Sport Psychology for Coaches.* Champaign: Human Kinetics.

Cale, L. and Harris, J. (2011). Learning about Health Through Physical Education and Youth Sport. In K. Armour (ed.), *Sport Pedagogy an Introduction for Teaching and Coaching.* Harlow: Prentice Hall, 53–64.

Canada Sport for Life Society (2016). *Physical Literacy.* Available at: http://canadiansportforlife.ca/ten-key-factors/physical-literacy (Accessed 2 August 2016).

Carney, P. and Howells, K. (2008). The Primary Physical Education Specialist. *Primary Physical Education Matters*, 3 (3), 35.

Carroll, B. and Loumidis, J. (2001). Children's Perceived Competence and Enjoyment in Physical Education and Physical Activity Outside School. *European Physical Education Review*, 7 (1), 24–43.

Chief Medical Officers (2011). *Start Active, Stay Active: A Report on Physical Activity for Health from the Four Home Countries.* London: Crown.

Coe, S. (2011). It Started with a Bid. *Sport* 217, 9 September, 19–26.

Department for Education (DfE) (2013). *The National Curriculum in England. Key Stages 1 and 2 Framework Document.* London: Crown.

Department for Education (DfE) (2013b). *Evidence on Physical Education and Sport in Schools.* London: Crown.

Department for Education (DfE) (2014). *Statutory Framework for the Early Years Foundation Stage. Setting the Standards for Learning, Development and Care for Children from Birth to Five.* London: Crown.

Department for Education (DfE) (2015). *Early Years Foundation Stage Profile 2016 handbook*, December 2015. London: Crown.

Department for Education (DfE) (2016). *Guidance PE and Sport Premium for Primary Schools.* London: Crown.

Department for Education and Employment (DfEE)/Qualifications and Curriculum Authority (QCA) (1999). *The National Curriculum. Handbook for Primary Teachers in England. Key Stages 1 and 2.* London: HMSO.

Department of Health (2005). *Choosing Activity: A Physical Activity Action Plan.* London: Crown.

Department of Health (2016). *Every Movement Counts.* Infographics on physical activity guidelines for children. London: Crown.

Dischler, P. A. (2010). *Teaching the 3 Cs: Creativity, Curiosity and Courtesy. Activities That Build a Foundation for Success.* Thousand Oaks, CA: Corwin, SAGE.

Doherty, J. and Brennan, P. (2007). *Physical Education and Development 3–11 a Guide for Teachers.* Abingdon, Oxen: Routledge, Taylor and Francis Group.

Doherty, J. and Brennan, P. (2014). Chapter 3 – Learning to Move and Moving to Learn. In J. Doherty and P. Brennan (eds), *Physical Education 5–11: A Guide for Teachers*, Abingdon: Routledge, 42–58.

Dyson, B. and Casey, A., eds (2012), *Cooperative Learning in Physical Education: A Research Based Approach* . London: Routledge.

Dyson, B., and Grineski, S. (2001). Using cooperative learning structures in physical education. *Journal of Physical Education, Recreation & Dance*, 72(2), 28–31.

Fairclough, S., Butcher, Z. and Stratton, G. (2008). Primary School Children's Health-enhancing Physical Activity Patterns: The School as a Significant Environment? *Education 3-13*, 36 (4), 371–81.

Gallahue, D. L. and Donnelly, F. C. (2003). *Developmental Physical Education for All Children*, Vol. 1. Champaign, IL: Human Kinetics.

Gallahue, D. L. and Ozmun, J. C. (2006). *Understanding Motor Development: Infants, Children, Adolescents, Adults*, 6th edn; international ed. New York: McGraw-Hill Crown.

Gibson, J. J. (2015). *The Ecological Approach to Visual Perception: Classic Edition.* New York; London: Psychology Press; Taylor and Francis Group.

Green, K. (2002). Physical Education and 'the Couch Potato Society' – Part one. *European Journal of Physical Education*, 7, 95–107.

Griffin, L. and Butler, J. (2005). *Teaching Games for Understanding: Theory, Research & Practice*. Champaign: Human Kinetics.

Gruber, J. (1986). Physical Activity and Self-esteem Development in Children: A Meta-analysis. In G. A. Stull and H. M. Eckert (eds), *Effects of Physical Activity on Children*. Champaign, IL: Human Kinetics, 330–48.

Harris, J. and Cale, L. (2006). Good Practice Guidelines in Physical Education Teacher Education. *British Journal of Physical Education*, Spring 2006.

Hastie, P. (2010). *Student Designed Games*. Champaign, IL: Human Kinetics.

Health and Safety Executive (2016). Available at http://www.hse.gov.uk/ (Accessed 31 October 2016).

Hellison, D. and Templin, T. (1991). *A Reflexive Approach to Teaching Physical Education*. Champaign, IL: Human Kinetics.

Howells, K. (2007). A Critical Reflection of the Opportunities and Challenges of Integrating the Every Child Matters (ECM) Agenda into teaching Physical Education (PE). *Primary Physical Education Matters*, 2 (1), ii–iii.

Howells, K. (2011). Chapter 7, An Introduction to Physical Education. In P. Driscoll, A. Lambirth and J. Roden (eds), *The Primary Curriculum: A Creative Approach*. London: SAGE, 118–36. http://dx.doi.org/10.1080/03004279.2016.1171572.

Howells, K. (2012). Chapter 13, Pacing an Importance on Health and Physical Activity. In G. Griggs (ed.), *An Introduction to Primary Physical Education.* London: Routledge, 207–20.

Howells, K. (2014). The contribution of the primary school setting and physical education lessons to children's physical activity levels. Doctoral Thesis, Canterbury Christ Church University. Available at http://create.canterbury.ac.uk/13301/

Howells, K. (2015). Physical Education Planning. In K. Sewell (ed.), *Planning the Primary National Curriculum: A Complete Guide for Trainees and Teachers*. Sage: London, 262–76.

Howells, K. (2016). Chapter 10, Supporting Physical Development, Health and Well-being Through the use of Outdoor Environments. In K. Ritchie (ed.), *Exploring Children's Learning: 3–11 years*, 142–60.

Howells, K. (2016). *Physical Development, Health and Well-being*. AIESEP (International Association of Colleges of Physical Education) International Conference, *Blazing New Trials: Future Directions for Sport Pedagogy and Physical Activity*, Wyoming, USA, June 2016.

Howells, K. and Bowen, J. (2016). *Physical Activity and Self-esteem: 'Jonny's Story'.* Education 3-13: International Journal of Primary. *Elementary and Early Years Education*, 44 (5), 577–90.

Howells, K. and Meehan, C. (2015). *Walking the Talk?* Thinking and Acting – Teachers' and Practitioners' Perceptions about Physical Activity, Health and Well-being, Do They 'Walk the Talk'. World Academy of Science, Engineering and Technology. *International Journal of Sport and Exercise Sciences*, 2 (5).

James, A. and Elbourn, J. (2016). *Safe Practice: In Physical Education, School Sport and Physical Activity*, 9th edn. Leeds: Coachwise.

Jess, M. and Dewar, K. (2004). Basic Moves, Developing a Foundation for Lifelong Physical Activity. *The British Journal of Teaching Physical Education*, 35 (2), 24–7.

Kinchin, G.D. and Bailey, R. (2010). *Physical Education: A Guide for Secondary Schools*. London: Continuum.

Kirk, D. (1993). Curriculum Work in Physical Education: Beyond the Objectives Approach? *Journal of Teaching in Physical Education*, 12 (3), 244–65.

Kirk, D. (1993). in R. Tinning, D. Kirk and J. Evans (1995). *Learning to Teach Physical Education*, Upper Saddle River, NJ, USA: Prentice Hall.

Kline, N. (1999). *Time to Think: Listening to Ignite the Human Mind*. London: Ward Lock.

Kohn, A. (1986). *No Contest: The Case Against Competition*. New York: Houghton Mifflin Company

Kolle, E., Steene-Johannessen, J., Klasson-Heggebø, L., Andersen, L. B. and Anderssen, S. A. (2009). A 5-yr Change in Norwegian 9-yr olds' Objectively Assessed Physical Activity Level. *Medicine and Science in Sports and Exercise*, 41 (7), 1368–73.

Laban, R. (1975). *Modern Educational Dance*. London: MacDonald and Evans.

Laker, A. (2000). *Beyond the Boundaries of Physical Education. Educating Young People for Citizenship and Social Responsibility*. London: Routledge.

Launder, A. (2001). *Play Practice: The Games Approach to Teaching and Coaching Sports*. Champaign, IL; Leeds: Human Kinetics.

Lavin, J., ed. (2008). *Creative Approaches to Physical Education: Helping Children to Achieve their True Potential*. London: Routledge.

Lawrence, J. (2012). *Teaching Primary Physical Education*. London: SAGE.

Lounsbery, M. A. F and McKenzie, T. L. (2015). Physically Literate and Physically Educated: A Rose by any other Name? *Journal of Sport and Health Science*, 4 (2), 139–44.

MacAllister, J. (2013). The 'Physically Educated' Person: Physical education in the philosophy of Reid, Peters and Aristotle, Educational Philosophy and Theory: *Incorporating ACCESS*, 45 (9), 908–20, doi: 10.1080/00131857.2013.785353.

Mawer, M (1990). It's not what you do – it's the way that you do it! Teaching Skills in Physical Education. *British Journal of Physical Education*, 21 (2), 307–31.

McKenzie, T. L. and Kahan, D. (2004). Impact of the Surgeon General's report: Through the Eyes of Physical Education Teacher Educators. *Journal of Teaching in Physical Education*, 23 (4), 300–17.

Meggit, C. (2006). *Child Development: An Illustrated Guide*. London: Heinemann Educational Publishers.

Metzler, M. W. (2011). *Instructional Models for Physical Education*, 3rd edn. Scottsdale, AZ: Holcomb Hathaway.

Miller, S. (1978). The facilitation of fundamental motor skill learning in young children. Unpublished doctoral dissertation. Michigan State University, Milligan.

Morgan, P. J. and Hansen, V. (2008). Physical Education in Primary Schools: Classroom Teachers' Perceptions of Benefits and Outcomes. *Health Education Journal*, 67 (3), 196–207.

Morley, D. and Bailey, R. (2006). *Meeting the Needs of your Most Able Pupils: Physical Education and Sport (Meeting the Needs of your Most Able Pupils)*. London: David Fulton Publishers.

Mosston, M. and Ashworth, S. (2002). *Teaching Physical Education. Theory, Practice and Research*, 5th edn. New York: Macmillan.

Murphy, F. and Ní Chroinin, D. (2011). Chapter 11 Playtime: The Needs of Very Young Learners in Physical Education and Sport. In K. Armour (ed.), *Sport Pedagogy*

An Introduction for Teaching and Coaching. London: Pearson Education Limited, 140–52.

NHS (National Health Service) (2011). *Physical Activity Guidelines for Children and Young People.* Available at: http://www.nhs.uk/Livewell/fitness/Pages/physical-activity-guidelines-for-young-people.aspx (Accessed 17 August 2011).

NHS (National Health Service) (2013). Physical activity guidelines for children and young people. Available at: http://www.nhs.uk/Livewell/fitness/Pages/physical-activity-guidelines-for-young-people.aspx (Accessed 15 July 2015).

OFSTED (2013). *Beyond 2012 – Outstanding Physical Education for all. Physical Education in Schools 2008–12.* Available at: https://www.ofsted.gov.uk/resources/120367 (Accessed 5 November 2016).

Pacific Institute for Sport Excellence (2016). What is Physical Literacy. Available at: http://piseworld.com/physical-literacy/(Accessed 2 August 2016).

Pickup, I. and Price, L. (2007). *Teaching Physical Education in the Primary School. A Developmental Approach.* London: Continuum.

Pickup, I., Price, L., Shaughnessey, J., Spence, J. and Trace, M. (2008). *Learning to Teach Primary PE.* London: SAGE. Learning Matters.

Public Health England (2014). *Everybody Active, Every Day. An Evidence Based Approach to Physical Activity.* Available at: https://www.gov.uk/government/uploads/system/uploads/attachment_data/file/374914/Framework_13.pdf

Public Health England (2015). *What Works in Schools and Colleges to Increase Physical Activity?* Available at https://www.gov.uk/government/uploads/system/uploads/attachment_data/file/469703/What_works_in_schools_and_colleges_to_increas_physical_activity.pdf (Accessed 20 November 2016).

Randell, V., Richardson, A., Swaithes, W. and Adams, S. (2016). *Generation Next: The Preparation of Pre-service Teachers in Primary Physical Education.* Winchester: University of Winchester.

Raymond, C. (1998). *Coordinating Physical Education Across the Primary School* (Subject leader's handbooks). London and Bristol, PA: Falmer Press.

Redelius, K., Quennerstedt, M. and Öhman, M. (2015). Communicating Aims and Learning Goals in Physical Education: Part of a Subject for Learning? *Sport, Education and Society,* 20 (5), 641–55.

Richardson, H. (2011). Britain's Pupils are Bad Losers, Survey Suggests. Available at: http://www.bbc.co.uk/news/education-12938578 (Accessed 30 April 2011).

Rink, J. E., Hall, T. J. and Williams, L. H. (2010). *Schoolwide Physical Activity.* Champaign, IL: Human Kinetics.

Royal Society for the Prevention of Accidents (2016). Available at: http://www.rospa.com/school-college-safety/teaching-safely/sport-leisure-water/ (Accessed 18 November 2016).

Russell, G. (1989). *Belief Systems Theory – A Process for Human Development.* Unpublished PhD Thesis. California University.

Sallis, J. and Owen, N. (1999). *Physical Activity and Behaviour Medicine.* Thousand Oaks: SAGE.

Shaughnessy, J. (2008). Chapter 5: Health and Safety: Guidelines for Good Practice, Resources to Support Teaching and Learning in PE. In I. Pickup, L. Price, J. Shaughnessy, J. Spence and M. Trace (eds), *Learning to Teach Primary PE.* London: SAGE Learning Matters.

Sheets-Johnstone, M. (2013). Movement as a Way of Knowing. *Scholarpedia,* 8 (6), 30375, doi:10.4249/scholarpedia.30375

Shields, D. L. and Bredemeier, B. L. (2009). *True Competition: A Guide to Pursuing Excellence in Sport and Society.* Champaign: Human Kinetics.

Shields, D. L. and Funk, C. (2011). Teach to Compete. *Strategies: A Journal for Physical and Sport Educators*, 24 (5), 8–11.

Shulman, L. (1987). Knowledge and Teaching: Foundations of the New Reform. *Harvard Educational Review*, 15, 4–22.

Siedentop, D. (1994). *Sport Education: Quality PE through Positive Sports Experiences.* Champaign: Human Kinetics.

Simons-Morton, B. G., Taylor, W. C., Snider, S. A., Huang, I. W. and Fulton, J. E. (1994). Observed Levels of Elementary and Middle School Children's Physical Activity during Physical Education Classes. *Preventative Medicine*, 23 (4), 437–41.

Skultety, S. (2011). Categories of Competition. *Sport, Ethics and Philosophy*, 5 (4), 433–46.

Slavin, R. (1995). *Cooperative Learning*, 2nd edn. Boston, MA: Allyn & Bacon.

Smith A. (2002). *Move It. Physical Movement and Learning.* Stafford, UK: Network Educational Press, Ltd.

Spitz, R. (1983). *Dialogues from Infancy*, edited by Robert N. Emde. New York: International Universities Press.

Sport Wales (2013). *Physical Literacy. A Journey Through Life.* Cardiff: Sport Wales.

Talbot, M. (2001). in T. Macfadyen and R. Bailey (2002). *Teaching Physical Education 11–18: Perspectives and Challenges.* London: Continuum.

Thorpe, R., Bunker, D. and Almond, L. (1982). *Rethinking Games Teaching.* Loughborough, England: Department of Physical Education and Sport Science, University of Technology.

Tinning, R. (2011). *Pedagogy and Human Movement: Theory, Practice, Research.* London and New York: Routledge.

Ward, H. and Roden, J. (2008). *Teaching Science in the Primary Classroom.* London: SAGE.

Welsh Assembly Government (2008). *Physical Development, Play, Learn, Grow, Cyfnod Sylfaen 3–7 Foundation Phase.* Cardiff: Crown.

Whitehead, M. E., ed. (2010). *Physical Literacy: Throughout the Lifecourse.* London: Routledge.

Whitlam, P. (2005). *Case Law in Physical Education and School Sport: A Guide to Good Practice.* Worcester: BAALPE.

Williams, A. (1996). *Teaching Physical Education a Guide for Mentors and Students.* London: David Fulton.

Williams, A. and Cliffe, J. (2011). *Primary PE: Unlocking the Potential.* Maidenhead: Open University Press.

Winsley, R. and Armstrong, N. (2005). Chapter 4, Physical Activity, Physical Fitness, Health and Young People. In K. Green and K. Hardman (eds), *Physical Education Essential Issues.* London: SAGE, 65–77.

Women in Sport (2016). *Changing the Game for Girls: In Action.* London: Women In Sport.

World Health Organization (WHO) (2010). *Global Recommendations on Physical Activity For Health.* Geneva, Switzerland: WHO Press.

Wright, R. (2010). *Multifaceted Assessment for Early Childhood Education.* Thousand Oaks, CA: Sage.

Yarnold, L. (2014). Lizzy Yarnold Olympic, World and European Champion. Available at http://lizzyyarnold.com/profile/ (Accessed 23 November 2016).

Yelling, M., Penney, D. and Swaine, I. L. (2000). Physical Activity in Physical Education: A Case Study Investigation. *European Journal of Physical Education*, 5 (1), 45–66.

Youth Sport Trust (2013). Level 2 and Level 3 Primary and Secondary Sport Formats. Available at: https://www.yourschoolgames.com/sports/level-23-sports (Accessed 31 October 2016).

Youth Sport Trust (2014). *Getting Girls Active. Impact Through Innovation.* London: Top Foundation.

Youth Sport Trust (2005). *TOPs Cards Teacher Resources*. Loughborough: Youth Sport Trust.

Youth Sport Trust (2016). https://www.youthsporttrust.org (Accessed 18 November 2016).

Index